1-2-3 MAGIC

IS AMERICA'S S
PARENTING PR

OVER 2 MILLION COPIES SOLD

MORE THAN 2 MILLION COPIES SOLD

1-2-3
MAGIC

The New **3-Step Discipline**
for Calm, Effective,
and Happy Parenting

·········· *Revised 6th Edition* ··········

THOMAS W.
PHELAN, PhD

NATIONAL PARENTING PUBLICATIONS AWARDS **GOLD WINNER**

WHAT PARENTS ARE SAYING ABOUT *1-2-3 MAGIC*:

"This book changed our lives."

"The ideas in this book work!
It really is like magic! I feel
like I am back in charge."

"My three-year-old has
become a different
little girl, and she is
so much happier now."

Praise for Tom W. Phelan, PhD, and 1-2-3 Magic

WHAT PARENTS ARE SAYING:

"This book **changed our lives.**"

"My three-year-old has become a different little girl, **and she is so much happier now.**"

"**The ideas in this book work!** It really is like magic! I feel like **I am back in charge.**"

"Simple, clear, concise, and **easy to follow.**"

"**I highly recommend this book** if you need a method of dealing with your little one(s) that keeps everyone calm."

"Extremely **helpful and informative.**"

"A **great book** for any parent!"

"**I was desperate for a change** in my family dynamics. **This book was the answer!**"

"**Fantastic book** that really helps with toddler tantrums. **My husband and I both read it,** and now **we are disciplining in the same way.** This book has been a **lifesaver!**"

"*1-2-3 Magic* simplifies everything I've read in other books, which makes it **very easy to follow.** Our home has become **a much more positive place.**"

"**Easy to read** and easy to follow."

"**Buy this book; read this book; follow the instructions in this book!** I highly recommend this to anyone involved in disciplining children."

"*1-2-3 Magic* **made parenting fun again.**"

"All I have to say is that **the ideas in this book WORK!** It really is like magic!"

"**This book is amazing!** My three-year-old was having major tantrums 4–6 times a day, screaming at the top of his lungs. After applying *1-2-3 Magic*, he rarely has meltdowns."

"*1-2-3 Magic* **takes the stress out of discipline.**"

"**It's such a relief to not feel like I'm constantly yelling at someone!** If you want to see a fast improvement in your child's behavior, check out *1-2-3 Magic*."

"Fantastic book that **really helps with my toddler's tantrums.**"

"This is the **one-stop, go-to book** that we have referred to time and again."

"This book is a great tool! It **helped me feel confident and proud of my parenting skills.**"

"The methods are described clearly, and they are **easy for any parent to follow.** I am **already seeing an improvement** in the way I react to my five- and seven-year-olds."

"We feel **more in charge** and **in control.**"

"**Saved my blood pressure** and my relationship with my kids."

"**This book isn't just about time-outs and discipline;** it encompasses an entire parenting philosophy."

"**I highly recommend this book** to any parent who is **spending more time yelling at or nagging** their children **than smiling at and laughing with them.**"

"**Thank you, Dr. Phelan,** for **sharing the results of your extensive research** and experimentation with the rest of the world!"

"*1-2-3 Magic* **saved my marriage.**"

"This is a **must-read** for all parents."

"Our little girl had gotten full-blown into the terrible twos and **I was desperate to get the calm back in my household.** She caught on to this method in one day. **Our house is a pleasant place to be again.**"

"This book **really helps!**"

"If you have challenges with your kids and you consistently follow the directions in this book, **you will have such a better relationship with your children.**"

"I have read many discipline books and tried many different methods. **This was the one that worked for our family.**"

"Thank you, Dr. Phelan! **You are a lifesaver!**"

WHAT EXPERTS ARE SAYING:

"**This book is easy to read and navigate.** As an in-home therapist I need lots of parent-friendly tools to use with families, and this is one of them. **I highly recommend it!**"

"As a parent and a school social worker, I highly recommend this book/system to everyone."

"**A wonderful book to use with parents in therapy** to assist with parenting skills."

"As a school guidance counselor, **I highly recommend this book** to both parents and teachers."

"Great book! **I am a pediatrician and I recommend it to my patients.**"

"**I've recommended this book for years** in my practice as a psychotherapist."

"**This is a staple** in my child therapy practice's pantry of goods."

"As a pediatrician, **I believe all caretakers should read** *1-2-3 Magic* and I cannot recommend it highly enough."

"As a mental health professional, I've found *1-2-3 Magic* to be **the most powerful method** of managing kids aged 2–12 that I've ever come across."

THE BEST MOMS *Don't* DO IT ALL

How Moms Got Stuck Doing Everything For Their Families and What They Can Do About It

Thomas W. Phelan, PhD.

Bestselling Author of *1-2-3 Magic*

Published by Sourcebooks
P.O. Box 4410, Naperville, Illinois 60567-4410
(630) 961-3900
sourcebooks.com

Originally published as *The Manager Mom Epidemic* in 2019 by Sourcebooks.

Cataloging-in-Publication Data is on file with the Library of Congress.

Printed and bound in the United States of America.
POD

CONTENTS

Do You Feel Like
the Family Nag?

D O YOU ENJOY BEING THE family nag? I'm sure you don't. But over the course of forty years working with families, I've observed a huge number of mothers (both those who work outside the home and those who don't) who spend most of their time every day managing the logistics of their families—shopping for and cooking meals, cleaning up, helping with homework, scheduling appointments, reminding their children and husbands to go to those appointments... It seems never-ending. Why do these moms take on all this work? Because they feel like if they don't do it, no one will—and the day-to-day functioning of the family will fall apart.

Does this sound like you? If so, you've come to the right place. Many American families are living with a condition I call the Manager Mom Syndrome, which is just what I described above: a household run almost exclusively by Mom. Why is that a bad thing? Well, Mom is tired. Mom is overwhelmed. Mom has her own life to live, and maybe she would like to do something with her free time other than attend to the details of her family members' lives. And the truth is that the best moms *don't* do it all.

Before we go any further, I must acknowledge that not every American family consists of the mom/dad/kids framework I use as the basis of this book. Many families are run by single parents. Many others are run by two women or by two men. Many families are formed through adoption, fertility assistance, or some other plan other than biological conception between two married, heterosexual adults. The diversity of the families in our country is something to be recognized and celebrated, and I hope that every type of parent finds something useful to take away from *The Best Moms Don't Do It All*. The content of this book is driven by normative data of large populations, which overwhelmingly shows that families headed by heterosexual parents fall into a pattern in which the woman handles the majority of the daily responsibilities. Much has been written in the past several years about the "mental load" or "emotional labor" that is borne by mothers, and this book is a contribution to that conversation. If you are a father who finds himself shouldering the majority of the burden, or you are in a same-sex relationship, I hope the concepts and takeaways of this book help you create a happier, more equal family, and that the language used throughout for convenience doesn't stand in the way of the benefits this book strives to provide.

So, what is the Manager Mom Syndrome? It is an unwitting conspiracy between Mom, Dad, and the kids, who all believe that, in general, if the work of running the household is going to get done *now* and get done *right*, Mom has to do it. The good news is that this belief isn't true, and the happiest families share the work and the fun equally without too much of the burden falling onto any single person.

So if you're tired of being the one who always schedules the dentist appointments, buys presents for birthday parties, and handles the emotional labor of remembering, planning, scheduling, reminding (and reminding again), it's time to fire Manager Mom. Let's get started!

What Does the Manager Mom Syndrome Feel Like?

Ella: "I'm so tired! I have to do everything by myself. I was up till eleven last night doing laundry, and that was after getting the kids to bed. My husband likes his alone time at night after working all day."

Hailey: It's 9:15 a.m. on a Saturday morning. Hailey has been up since 5:30 a.m. entertaining and feeding her two kids, two-month-old Carter and fourteen-month-old Owen. Husband Grant is still asleep, snoring peacefully. Hailey resolves that next week she is going to find more time for herself, one way or another. Will her husband want breakfast when he gets up? Why can't he get his own?

Aubrey: At least sixty times per day, Aubrey wonders whether or not she is a good mother. She remembers hearing a speaker once who mentioned a concept known as "total motherhood." This was the idea that all the responsibilities for child-rearing rested solely on the shoulders of the mother of the house. Aubrey feels that's the way things are in her home. She has one child, five-year-old Taylor, but her husband spends time with the child only on the weekends, and that's mainly engaging in fun activities—not the childcare basics such as bathing, dressing, feeding, and so on.

Abigail: "I'd love to go out at night, but I can't imagine just being gone from home for three hours straight. And I can tell you this, I'd feel really funny just announcing that I'm leaving the house for a long time for the sole purpose of hanging out with a friend."

Kylie: Kylie is hunkered down at a motel just eight miles from her home. She told her family she was taking a week off and going "on strike." She left her husband, eight-year-old daughter, and twelve-year-old son at home to fend for themselves. Kylie explained, while trying to suppress her resentment, that she was tired of being what she called the "family gopher." Cook, babysitter, laundromat manager, picker-upper, toilet scrubber, scheduler, chauffeur—you name it. Secretly, Kylie hopes the family will feel an appropriate sense of guilt, come to appreciate all the services Mom has offered, and change their ways when she returns from her "vacation."

Janelle: "Friday is my laundry day. I get it started after I get home from work. Do you think the kids—and Dad—can take the time from their busy schedules to get their stuff down to the laundry room? Guess again—no, don't think so. I nag and nag, which I don't enjoy, then half the time I have to get their dirty clothes myself."

No One Is Happy

Although you might think that Mom might be the only one upset about Manager Mom Syndrome, everyone in the family has issues with these Mom-directs-all scenarios. Kids don't like being told what to do all the time, and they become more uncooperative, forgetful, and resistant the more nagging they hear. (Psychologists sometimes call this "passive-aggressive" behavior.) Dad gets tired of

Everyone in the family has issues with these Mom-directs-all scenarios.

listening to arguments between his spouse or partner and the children, and he tends to pull back and—in some ways—"disappear." How long does it take to read the sports page in the bathroom?

Of course, the biggest victim of the Manager Mom Syndrome is Mom. In this kind of family set-up, Mom justifiably feels taken advantage of and overloaded. Mothers—particularly those with small children—feel anxious ("Can we get all the chores done today?"), resentful ("Why doesn't anyone around here help out?"), guilty ("Am I a good mom?"), and depressed ("Is this my life?"). *Mom's mental health takes a beating.*

As one mother put it, "With all these people and all this activity, *I feel as though I've lost myself.*" How? Here's one example. In 1980, Gerald R. Patterson wrote a paper called *Mothers: The Unacknowledged Victims.* That book was written, surprisingly, *before* a lot of mothers started working outside the home part-time and then, more and more, full-time. Patterson pointed out, after extensive research, that mothers of normal preschoolers are regularly exposed to "high densities of aversive events."[1] In other words, raising these cute little creatures—pretty much alone—is a tough and often unpleasant job.

Arlie Hochschild's well-known work, *The Second Shift: Working Families and the Revolution at Home,* originally published in 1989, highlighted another version of the stress on moms.[2] Hochschild pointed out that even when men and women both worked outside the home, women tended to do a "second shift" on evenings and weekends that included taking care of *most* of the primary childcare, secondary childcare, and housework responsibilities.

In her 2018 book, *Fed Up: Emotional Labor, Women, and the Way Forward*, Gemma Hartley adds another twist to this picture by describing how the current domestic scenario actually adds insult to injury for mothers. First of all, direct, primary childcare is usually a very difficult kind of mental or "emotional labor."[3] Though it has its rewards, it is also a kind of unremitting and lonely drudgery. Second, primary childcare with very young kids does not receive anywhere near the kind of social support and recognition that working outside the home provides.

What Is the Manager Mom Syndrome?

When all is said and done, the Manager Mom Syndrome is a kind of maternal addiction, and Dad, partner, and kids are the passive enablers of the obsession. Oddly enough—and you can look at the problem through different lenses—Mom is often addicted to an occupation that has a number of positive descriptors: President, Servant, Commander, Crisis Manager, and First Responder, for example, come to mind. Those roles are usually considered positive ones.

But in filling these roles, Manager Mom *overdoses* on kindness, helpfulness, organizational skills, and commitment to getting the work done. In the process of expressing these normally constructive traits, *Mom loses her healthy free time—and herself.*

What about the enablers—the other members of the family? Well, if Mom wants to take responsibility for everything, fine! Often other family members will simply let Mom take over, thus unwittingly and inadvertently sacrificing their own independence and competence.

When the Manager Mom Syndrome goes untreated and the behavior of its active (moms) and passive (dads and kids) conspirators continues unchecked, the Syndrome sometimes morphs into its absolute worst expression: *Martyr Mom*. This condition is especially difficult to deal with, because among its symptoms is the fact that as time passes—more and more—the participants in the drama start to *enjoy their own misery*.

Fortunately, Manager Mom Syndrome is a curable condition. For that remedy to materialize, though, both moms and dads need to hear some things they don't really want to hear. Then both moms and dads need to do some things that they might not really want to do—at least for a while. And—surprise, surprise—the kids have to be included in some meaningful way. The process can sometimes be extremely difficult, but the effort is usually worth it. Living in a household where Mom's angry organizational dominance and constant supervision seem to be a requirement for smooth operation is not good for *anyone's* mental health or for the happiness of the family as a whole.

CHAPTER SUMMARY

Three Concepts
▸ Kid's Independence
▸ Equal Suffering Law
▸ Family Bonding

Eradicate Manager MOM!

PART I

HOW DID WE GET HERE?

The Origins and Side Effects of Manager Mom

ONE

Interpersonal Bonding vs. the Frantic Modern Family

ONCE MANAGER MOM IS IN operation, its side effects start reinforcing the Syndrome itself, locking everyone into a kind of powerful and self-perpetuating vicious circle. In this chapter, we'll take a look at the *family bonding* part of the Manager Mom problem.

Warmth and Affection: Goals

One of the deepest and most universal human needs is to have close and affectionate relationships with the people you live with. That means to both *know* them and to *like* them. In my experience, the vast majority of high school students admit to wanting a good family life in the future.

One of the deepest and most universal human needs is to have close and affectionate relationships with the people you live with.

Now, if normally oppositional teens admit to such a need, it must be a powerful one!

This future interpersonal goal of adolescents is right on the money for good reason. In addition to finding other people fun and enjoyable to be with, volumes of research consistently indicate that *both physical and mental health are much better when people experience warm and friendly connections at home.*

As part of their goal to live happily with others, the vast majority of human beings also want to become parents. They want to raise a couple of those adorable little tykes. Having children and becoming a parent does provide a deep sense of meaning and purpose to the lives of many people. Whether they actually have them or not, about 95 percent of adults say they want (or did want) children.[4] That's an amazingly universal statistic! In fact, if you are in the business of dating and you *don't* want to have kids, it is considered very bad form to not reveal your preference early on in any relationship.

Warmth and Affection: Realities

In spite of this universal goal and deep desire for affectionate, live-in family relationships, we humans don't seem to be very skilled at getting what we want. When it comes to family affection, warmth, and bonding, we don't seem to do well at all. Look at these data:

- 41 percent of first marriages end in divorce.
- 60 percent of second marriages end in divorce.

- 73 percent of third marriages end in divorce.[5]

This is really sad. All of us want closeness and affection at home, but we don't seem to be very good at achieving that goal. What, specifically, is going wrong, and does the Manager Mom Syndrome relate to whatever is causing the trouble? Let's examine the process by which most of us create our families.

Step 1. Finding Mr. or Ms. Right

If you're like most people, somewhere in your adolescent or post-adolescent years you came across another person whom you thought was fun to be with. Your mutual activities involved doing lots of fun things (dating) and probably also involved lots of genuine two-way conversations—often until early into the morning. After a short while, it's very likely that your relationship also started including the potential narcotic: sex.

All this horsing around may have triggered in you another instinct that we refer to as *falling in love*. Falling in love refers to a mental state characterized by a desire to be with another person constantly, a tendency to idealize that other person, and a deep conviction that if you could ever live with that other person full-time you'd never have another care in the world again. This wonderful mental state, which psychologist Dorothy Tennov called "limerence," lasts, on average, about two years.[6]

Whether or not you actually felt like you were in love (not all do), during this dating process you were bonding with another human being:

1. Your experiences with them were by far mostly positive.

2. These pleasant experiences were frequent.

3. They were mutual and often very intense.

4. These positive experiences could last for long periods of time.

During this period, your new relationship cast a cheery glow over the rest of your life. After being apart for a while, your greetings were energetically warm, intense, and friendly, and you actively sought to maximize your time with each other.

Step 2. More!

You were now ready to make a monumental decision: The decision to live together or get married. Off you go! Though you did not know it at the time, as far as the health of your relationship went, this is one of the most dangerous decisions anyone can make. Studies consistently show that after getting married or starting to live together, a person's satisfaction with both their partner and their relationship begins its first steady decline (the second decline will come in just a bit).

Most of us, however, at the time we get married or move in are not thinking along these lines. Our thoughts go more like this: "Just think how much fun we're having now. And we're not even together all the time! After we live in the same home and pursue the same dreams, our fun will double or even triple. Wow—I can't wait!"

Moving in or getting married does have its rewards. There's no problem getting together anymore, and now you don't have to split up every night! But there's a catch.

Step 3. The Catch Part I

The happily-ever-after scenario is about to stumble over an unpleasant truth: your decision to live together will transform your relationship by altering its fundamental premise. While dating was a decision to *have fun together*, living together or getting married is unwittingly a decision to *work* together. Now we'll try to get ahead, we'll buy cars, we'll find a nice place to live, we'll get sick and care for one another, visit the families, and do the chores.

There is no guarantee that a good partner for *fun* will make a good partner for *work*. A fun-to-work switch like this might take the wind out of any relationship's sails—and, of course, it often does. Gradually—and sometimes not so gradually—the time spent on work, shopping, in-laws, finances, and everything else starts eating away at the time spent enjoying each other's company. The Household Heavy Hitters—laundry, food and drink preparation, kitchen cleanup, housecleaning, and household management—start to take their toll. You wake up one morning, look over at the person in bed next to you, and think, "You're not as much fun as you used to be."

You did not expect this change. Admit it—a large part of you hoped for Happily Ever After. Even if you had been aware of the research on the decline in marital satisfaction, it's likely you would have felt sure those negative trends would not apply to *you*.

So what happened? In pursuing all your dreams, the priority of work (shared tasks and separate tasks) replaced the priority of shared fun. Your experiences with one another changed to this:

1. The mutual experiences were less positive.
2. The positive experiences were less frequent.
3. The good experiences were less intense.
4. The upbeat experiences lasted for shorter periods of time.

In addition, for many couples, move-in time is when the Manager Mom Syndrome begins to creep into the picture. Most people moving in together have full-time jobs, but now they *potentially share* the Household Heavy Hitters: laundry, food and drink preparation, kitchen cleanup, housecleaning, and household management.

In my experience, where a guy has been on his own for a number of years, he is more likely to continue to do his own laundry and to enjoy cooking and some shopping. He is less likely to clean the kitchen and much less likely to clean the house (dust, vacuum, scrub toilets, etc.). With these problems men are not as likely to be First Responders. Women *are likely* to be First Responders, and in the absence of Constructive Household Division of Labor Negotiations (which usually do *not* occur), more tasks are likely to "default" to the female of the species.

In fact, at move-in time, many women are thrilled to do laundry for two, shop for two, cook for two, clean the kitchen, and clean the house. The "for two" part is fun, and it represents a milestone in life. The new man of the house thinks *This is cool!* and he reverts to a more traditional, household-passive male role. After not too long, however, the new milestone becomes an old millstone for his wife or partner, who begins to feel that she is always rushing frantically from chore to chore.

Step 4. The Catch Part 2: And Baby Makes Three

Unfortunately, at this developmental stage, Reality is not done with you: things are about to get tougher. The vast majority of adults choose to have children. In our culture, we romanticize having kids. The cover of your favorite magazine trumpets, "Superstar Actress Carrie Jones Expecting Twins! She's So Excited!!"

Adults produce children in response to one or more of a whole collection of positive images that evoke upbeat and pleasant feelings:

- Giving your parents grandchildren
- Reading a story at bedtime and snuggling
- Carrying on your family
- Social pressure/expectations
- Giving and receiving love
- Coaching your child's baseball team
- Embodying your love for one another
- Etc.

Earlier I mentioned that in this book you will hear some things you don't want to hear. Here's another unfortunate fact: *Having children speeds up the drop in marital or relationship satisfaction.*[7] A lot.

Over the first four years of marriage, for example, the decline in marital satisfaction for parents is double that for nonparents. The negative effects of that cute little bundle of joy are sudden and persistent, and studies show that it is mainly living at home with the children that interferes with adults' sense of well-being. Kids, in other words, are very hard to live with even if they are "cute as the dickens" and we love them very much.

Having kids is a thousand times easier said than done, but *not one of us* appreciates that reality beforehand. You simply can't. Many couples still believe,

> *Over the first four years of marriage, for example, the decline in marital satisfaction for parents is double that for nonparents.*

as a matter of fact, that having a baby will bring them closer together. But bringing the new child home is a kind of new awakening that causes permanent and revolutionary changes.

With the arrival of a first child, both parents lose a ton of their autonomy. A crying baby is no fun, and neither is getting up in the middle of the night. After going through what amounts to major surgery to have the child, Mom is tired all the time. Dad feels like he has lost his best friend—his wife. There's less or no sex. The baby is always there! Couples tend to inevitably take their "baby frustrations" out on each other, and they also say and do fewer pleasurable things to and for each other after the baby arrives.[8]

Manager Mom Syndrome Intensifies

In short, bringing home that first baby is traumatic for a couple. With a new baby, the change in the basis of the relationship from fun to work accelerates, the workload itself mushrooms, and mom-dad bonding suffers accordingly.

With diapers, feedings, laundry, and other childcare items, the Manager Mom phenomenon starts to emerge as mothers respond to the handling of these items much more naturally and spontaneously than dads do. Sleep deprivation also makes Mom's plight worse, since mothers are also more likely to attend to kids' bedtime and nighttime waking problems.

As kids get older, behavioral issues will add to parental and marital stress. One parental problem is controlling negative behavior, and another issue is encouraging good behavior. As happens with housework, Mom is usually more on the front lines than Dad when it comes to managing the following:

Negative Behavior	Positive Behavior
Arguing	Bedtime
Yelling	Homework
Whining	Getting up and out in the morning
Teasing	Chores
Tantrums	Eating
Pouting	Picking Up
Lying	Sleeping through the night
Sibling rivalry	Bathing and brushing teeth

Some writers feel that child behavior problems may be the number one cause of arguments between parents. Child discipline squabbles can also be aggravated by the fact that many times *neither* parent has any idea what he or she is doing when it comes to behavior management!

Bonding and the Frantic Modern Family

All this work-related and child-related stress often makes for a rushed and frantic household. What happens to the mom-dad bonding? A couple's affection for one another is still there, but it's weaker and it's not getting strengthened as often or as intensely as it used to. The warmth of the parent's relationship with each other no longer casts a cheerful glow over the rest of each person's life. After time apart, greetings are less energetic, warm, or friendly, and this change is noticeable to other people. Finally, maximizing time together is no longer a priority for moms and dads. It may not even be an issue anymore, since there is a good chance that both spouses or partners feel overdosed on family—including the baby.

What about parent-child bonding? Our data here present us with a strange paradox. As we saw, about 95 percent of adults say they want (or would have wanted) children, and in spite of all the stresses kids bring, a similar percentage of parents say they would have children again if they had the choice. In other words, having kids responds to a deep human need and adds profound meaning to an adult's life. The vast majority of parents love their kids very much.

The paradox, however, is that *in spite of that love and that profound meaning, living with and bonding with kids is problematic and stressful.* In one study, for example, researchers asked 909 working women what activities gave them the most pleasure.[9] Out of nineteen possible activities, childcare ranked low—sixteenth out of nineteenth (right behind housework).

In another study, parents were asked, "Whose company do you enjoy most?"[10] Here, children came in last behind friends, spouses, relatives, acquaintances, and one's own parents. Being with one's children was ranked the same as being with strangers.

For parents, in other words, kids are a "high-reward, high-cost" phenomenon.[11] One of the costs is a couple's transition from being lovers to being parents. Another cost is the change in focus from enjoying each other to getting all the work done. Both of those changes go a long way toward explaining why we

For parents, in other words, kids are a "high-reward, high-cost" phenomenon.

humans aren't so good at family bonding. To sustain a relationship, you need to play hard with your friend, lover, or child on a regular basis. Modern family life doesn't leave much time for fun—especially when Manager Mom Syndrome takes over.

Mom-dad bonding issues and parent-child bonding issues are a big part of the vicious cycle that is the Manager Mom Syndrome. So is another issue we call the Equal Suffering Law, which we'll examine next.

CHAPTER SUMMARY

Our culture tends to unrealistically romanticize the notion of having children. Why? Because adults don't like to feel like they're criticizing innocent little kids and also because children can be so cute and loveable. But the side effects of having little ones are a huge part of the Manager Mom problem.

TWO

The Equal Suffering Law:
Moms vs. Dads

OVER THE YEARS, WHENEVER I'VE mentioned The Equal Suffering Law (ESL) at parenting seminars, I always get the same response: knowing looks, subdued laughter, and some scattered, sheepish expressions—usually from the men. I used to think I would have to explain the concept, but it seems the audience was always one step ahead of me. I recently also discovered a book called *The Fairness Instinct*, which describes a basic human instinct or orientation toward equality or fair-mindedness.

The Equal Suffering Law applies to all families, and it's as old as the hills. Here's a definition: The ESL is my term for the human belief or rule that in any meaningful and relatively permanent group, people *should* work or contribute equally to the extent they are able. Individuals are expected to put forth equal amounts of effort (which can include discomfort or pain) in their attempts to provide for the common welfare of their group. People who do not contribute equally are known as *cheaters* (in evolutionary psychology terms) and these people are resented unless they are unable to perform their duties (e.g., very young children, the sick, or infirm).

The Family Division of Labor

Imagine a family with two children and two parents. Both parents are working full-time outside the house. Marriages where both parents work now make up more than two-thirds of all marriages that involve children.[12] In the history of mankind both parents working outside the house like this represents an unusual situation. It is a decidedly modern phenomenon.

Let's also imagine a big list of all the things that have to be done around the house where these two parents and two children are living. There are lots of different ways to describe and categorize what needs to be done, but let's assume that our to-do list involves several categories: Childcare Basics, Household Tasks, and Child Discipline:

Childcare Basics

Supervision	Hygiene	Grooming
Safety	Potty Training	
Feeding	Dressing	

Household Tasks

Cooking	Doing yard work	Making beds
Taking care of pets	Recycling	Cleaning bathrooms
Scheduling car maintenance	Watering plants	Managing money
Shopping (food, clothes, school supplies)	Doing dishes	Cleaning kitchen
Doing laundry	Dusting	Vacuuming
Straightening up	Cleaning bedrooms	
Scheduling activities (friends, family)	Taking out garbage	

Child Discipline

Arguing	Lying	Sleeping through the night
Yelling	Adhering to bedtime	Bathing
Whining	Doing homework	Brushing teeth
Teasing	Getting up and out	
Tantrums	Eating	
Pouting	Picking up	

These lists define for this family exactly *what the common welfare is.* Now recall that the Equal Suffering Law requires (or strongly suggests, anyway) that each person contribute equally to the common welfare to the extent that they are able. The classic ESL problem is that Manager Mom is doing too many things from this list, and Dad is not doing enough. Therefore, Dad

> **The Equal Suffering Law requires that each person contribute equally to the common welfare to the extent that they are able.**

is put into evolutionary psychology's *cheater* category, and Mom is resentful. Violations of the fair division of labor, in fact, are a huge issue in many marriages, help explain our high divorce rate, and account for a ton of mom-dad bonding issues.

Years ago, in *The Second Shift*, for example, Hochschild quoted a study by Alexander Szalai that triggered a lot of controversy. Szalai in 1966 found that working women spent three hours per day doing housework while men averaged 17 minutes.[13] Women averaged fifty minutes per day with the kids, men twelve minutes. On the leisure side, men watched TV for an average of one hour per day longer than their wives and slept one half hour more every night.

Over the last several decades, there has been a steady increase in the amount of time males contribute to the common welfare, aside from the income they produce from their outside work. This increase includes greater time spent on the Household Heavy Hitters (most time-consuming), such as food and drink preparation, kitchen and food cleanup, interior cleaning, laundry, and other household tasks. Dads are also doing more primary and secondary childcare (secondary childcare involves children under age thirteen in your care, but as the parent or caregiver, you can be doing another primary activity, such as housework, and not be directly caring for the child).

Surprisingly for some men and women, many men have reported actually enjoying these activities! And men doing more housework and childcare has meant a significant decrease in the severity of Manager Mom Syndrome in many households—a welcome change for the moms involved. In families where both parents work full-time, however, surveys usually find that women still spend more time doing household tasks, direct primary childcare, and secondary childcare.

The Second Shift, though, triggered a furor that still continues today. Interestingly, discussions about the fair division of labor around the house usually focus on Mom's work/effort vs. Dad's work/effort. Most of the time, what the children are doing or not doing is not involved in the discussion. That is a problem that we'll turn to in the next chapter.

Who's Going to Do What? Warriors and Worriers

So we have our big list of activities and chores that define the common family welfare and we have Mom vs. Dad inequities in labor output. How do problems with the Equal Suffering Law arise? Let's look at two critical elements, one psychological and one cultural.

The Psychological Element

In her book, *Warriors and Worriers: The Survival of the Sexes,* Joyce F. Benenson describes several innate, evolutionary, psychological differences between men and women. As warriors, she says, men are more oriented toward protecting the family from outside dangers, and they enjoy being with other men for the purposes of taking part in or watching sports, completing tasks, beating each other up, or actually engaging in war. As worriers, Benenson says, women have a different profile. When with other women, they enjoy talking more than men do. What do they talk about? Worries, what's wrong with their lives, personal vulnerabilities, and relationship issues.

Benenson describes other man/woman differences that apply to our present discussion of the ESL. Men "invest more in competing for females and initiating sex."[14] Women, she adds, "wisely exercise caution before they have sex and get stuck feeding and caring for the baby that emerges from their body." Women also "spend more time, energy, and resources in making sure the resulting baby stays alive." Women, according to *Warriors and Worriers*, typically spend more time caring for babies and older family members and finding and preparing food.

In Benenson's opinion, these traits are not to be seen as excuses for anyone's behavior, but rather as distinct behavioral tendencies that distinguish the two sexes. One of her conclusions takes us straight to a big part of the Equal Suffering Law problem: "Men like to take care of babies and children too, of course," she says, "but not as freely, frequently, or intensely as females do." The key here is in these three words:

Freely

Frequently

Intensely

This is another way of saying First Responder. Go back and look at our Household Tasks and Childcare Basics lists. Who's going to do what? Based on *her* evolutionary predispositions, Mom is going to respond to problems like dirty diapers, teeth brushing, feeding, and nighttime waking often before Dad is aware that anything needs to be done. What will Dad's reaction then be? Based upon *his* evolutionary predispositions, Dad's reaction will be: "Cool—I can live like this!"

This is why the difficulties of the new-baby transition are particularly hard on mothers. Moms respond first according to their traditional—or evolutionary—gender roles, and dads follow along passively.[15] Even when both spouses work outside the home (and there's the rub!), women take on more childcare and housework responsibilities.[16] As First Responders, the women may not like doing as much as they do, but their natural response is take care of certain problems, such as childcare or housework, when they see them.

Neither male nor female is trying to be malicious in creating the Manager Mom Syndrome. They are just doing their age-old, hereditary, evolutionary thing. In addition, though, and making matters worse, neither sex is adept at negotiating the ESL. The gals complain from time to time, the guys avoid the subject, and there are periodic blow-ups that accomplish nothing other than splitting the couple further apart.

The Cultural Element

So one contributor to ESL violations is psychological and evolutionary. The other is more recent, and it is cultural. The culture we live in no longer supports the kind of arrangement depicted in *The Second Shift*. In the 1950s, with fewer women working, it may have, but not anymore. Equal work/equal suffering and sharing the loads (childcare and housework) is the word on the street—and at home—today.

But even in the 1950s, before so many women started working full-time outside the home, something was wrong with the division-of-labor picture. Let's look at that for a second. Imagine in 1955 a dad who left home at 7:30 a.m. for work as an advertising copywriter. He got home at 5:30 p.m. The mom stayed home caring for kids who were aged two, five, and seven. When they all reconvened at 5:30 p.m., who had had the harder day, Mom or Dad?

The popular wisdom and culture at the time always claimed it was the father. After all, he was out there competing in the big, bad, dangerous world and it was his efforts that supported the entire family financially. But as Patterson pointed out long ago in *Mothers: The*

Unacknowledged Victims, the truth is that the mother had the harder day. Why? Both jobs, parenting and copywriting, were stressful and required high energy outputs. But Dad's job very likely provided more reward points, more meaningful challenges, fewer senseless interruptions, and work with adults. All-day parenting is not the same at all. As one frustrated mother once told me, "It's hard to spend all day with the kids. It's crazy! They're not the same age as me!" This, of course, is especially true when preschoolers are involved.

Even in the 1950s, Dad would not have traded places with Mom for anything. Sure, there are more stay-at-home dads today, but the numbers are still relatively small.

Recall the study asking moms what activities were most pleasurable for them. Kids came in sixteenth out of nineteen pursuits—right after housework. This may be why, in countries where subsidized childcare is readily available (e.g., Sweden, Finland), parenting satisfaction is higher than it is in the U.S. Moms often need more of a break!

The ESL: Keeping Score

Couples, of course, have different ways of keeping a tally of the status of the Equal Suffering Law in their house. In families where Dad works full-time and Mom works part-time, for example, childcare and housework labor discrepancies are not always seen as violations of the ESL. Mom may do more housework, primary childcare, and secondary childcare (like babysitting) without minding too much since they aren't spending as much time working outside the home as their partner is.

But determining how "fair" the distribution of labor is can get complicated. In fact, each of the following items has, at one time or another, been used for the purposes of comparison to tally up the ESL bottom line: hours spent at work, income from those hours, hours spent at home on housework/childcare irrespective of outside work, amount of leisure time available (especially on weekends), the difficulty of the tasks involved ("suffering"), and the amount of time spent thinking or worrying about particular jobs or concerns.

As you can easily imagine, it makes matters more difficult when each partner in a relationship has different criteria for calculating their Equal Suffering Law scores. If Dad and Mom both work full-time outside the house, for instance, but Dad makes twice as much income as Mom, Dad may feel that he is entitled to put in less time at home on housework and childcare. Mom may totally disagree. On the other hand, if both parents work full-time, Mom makes more than Dad, and Mom spends significantly more time on housework and childcare, we would obviously have a major violation of the fair distribution of labor!

Another interesting ESL calculation difficulty occurs in this way. For many Manager Moms themselves, *worrying about* household or child-related items is definitely part of the work/suffering/stress they feel on a regular basis. This worrying, thinking, and planning is what author Gemma Hartley defines as "emotional labor." GOOD! In fact, actual worrying can take up many hours per week at work, at home, or while driving around in the car. As we saw in Benenson's book, dads in general do not worry as much about domestic, family, or relationship matters as moms do. The fact that Dad may be less worried about the children than Mom, however, can cause resentment from Mom because she perceives Dad's "indifference" as a lack of caring *and* as an ESL violation.

Complicating matters further, adults tend to perceive the effort they expend on the common welfare in different but predictable ways. Both sexes *overestimate* the amount of work they do and *underestimate* their partner's contributions. After having been in the ESL "doghouse" for many years, dads more often perceive that there exists

> Dads more often perceive that there exists an equal distribution of labor on various tasks, while moms disagree and feel they are still doing more.

an equal distribution of labor on various tasks, while moms disagree and feel they are still doing more. It rarely goes the other way around. When ESL disagreements about who's doing what occur, who is usually a bit more accurate? The moms.[17]

With different people and different rules, keeping track of the Equal Suffering Law in a household is, as we have seen, not easy. In fact, it may be impossible most of the time. For many adults, even the mention of the phrase is distasteful and comes across as cheap, demeaning, or anything but altruistic. "Our relationship should be above that kind of scorekeeping!" many people feel. The ESL and the human sense of fairness, however, are a deep part of evolved human nature and are very real. It may be hard to arrive at any kind of accurate tally in any one family, but humans will always try!

In many families a close-to-equal distribution of labor in a fairly stable relationship is good enough. When Manager Mom Syndrome exists, however, ESL violations will *always* be part of the picture and they will result in significant marital stress. These violations will also tax Mom's mental health a good deal. Why? Because with the exception of Martyr Moms, most women do not feel good about themselves

Any good solution to the Manager Mom Syndrome has to involve significant contributions not just from dads, but also from the children.

when they dislike their own husbands. The issue must be addressed.

Who did we leave out of our ESL discussion here? We left out the people who are usually left out: the kids. Division of labor debates are usually about moms vs. dads. You'll soon see, however, that any good solution to the Manager Mom Syndrome has to involve *significant* contributions not just from dads, but also from the children. The good news, however, is that kids—with the help of their parents—can contribute to the common welfare and help eradicate Manager Mom Syndrome in several truly meaningful ways.

CHAPTER SUMMARY

People argue about whether or not the above differences in male and female behavior are primarily genetic or primarily cultural. Does it really make any difference? Isn't the most important issue what to do about the Manager Mom Epidemic!?

WAKEFUL STATE UNIVERSITY

THREE

Children's Independence vs. Chronic Supervision

T HE COLLEGE DEAN LOOKED OUT at his audience. Over five hundred excited, incoming first-year students and their parents looked back at him.

"I want to start by asking you parents a question," he began. "How many of you during the last year were still waking up your kids for school in the morning?" After a somewhat protracted pause, about half of the parents rather sheepishly raised their hands.

"As of today," he said, "you won't be doing that anymore. That's because you simply can't. And if your sons and daughters are interested, I'll be selling alarm clocks in the auditorium lobby after this presentation."

Independence Deficit Disorder

This is not an unusual school and these are not unusual parents or kids. But there is a big problem on display here that is typical of most families in this country, whether we're talking about families with two parents or partners, single parents, or families where a grandparent or other caretaker is raising the children. The problem is intimately tied up with the Manager Mom Syndrome, and in many ways it involves our basic philosophy of parenting. You might call it IDD—Independence Deficit Disorder.

IDD!
Independence Deficit Disorder

We are not training our kids to be independent. That means *independent of us—their parents.* Kids' autonomy is just not a priority for adults—we hardly give it a thought. We keep prompting, reminding, and nagging our kids with virtually no thought regarding: 1) how they react to this chronic supervision and 2) what they might really be capable of at their age. Manager Mom is usually the most active supervisor.

Thus, parents wake up eighteen-year-old seniors for school in the morning, then tell them to get some breakfast, and then make sure they have everything they need for school—including their math worksheet. Does a typically developing eighteen-year-old have the self-control and executive functioning capability to bring all this off on their own? What do you think? You probably think they can. What does Manager Mom think? She worries that her daughter will mess up. What does Dad think? He doesn't worry about it because Mom already does. This cycle of chronic supervision causes predictable and serious damage to kids, parents, and relationships.

What Is Our Priority?

Teaching our children to be *competently independent* should be our long-term goal. After all, we want our kids ultimately to get rid of us! But if our youngster's independence is not our goal, what is? Our daily goal is a more immediate and compelling—but short-term—goal: *Getting the work done now and getting it done right.* And we fly by the seat of our pants trying to accomplish this objective. Waking the kids up, getting them their breakfast, picking out their clothes, getting them off to school, fixing them dinner, seeing that they do their homework, getting them to bed, and—finally—making sure they stay in bed. No matter their age.

And what's our chief tactic for getting all this stuff done? Usually it's some form of more or less constant parental chatter. We expect our kids to respond cheerfully and cooperatively to our commands.

This scenario, basically, means that we see our children every day as *a series of jobs that need to get done or a series of problems that need to be solved.* We do not see our kids as people to be enjoyed. After all, they do have homework, they must eat, and they have to get sleep. True, the weekend may have an outing or two where the main purpose is to have fun together, but those events are counterbalanced by chauffeuring responsibilities, tasks such as cleaning, laundry, shopping, and other errands. Not to mention the never-ending child discipline issues such as arguing, yelling, disrespect, not eating, not cleaning rooms, and sibling rivalry.

Does this scenario sound familiar? It should. It's basically *the*

We see our children every day as a series of jobs that need to get done or a series of problems that need to be solved.

same *fun-to-work switch* that we encountered when we went from dating (having fun together) to moving in to the same place (working together).

This switch, you will recall, is the basis for the beginning of the decline in a couple's relationship satisfaction. We no longer see our partners so much as lovers and or playmates, but more as *people who can help get all the work done*. What is more, as we saw last chapter, our "partners" had better contribute their fair share to the common welfare!

What Are We Missing?

The kids. Our family is no longer just two partners or spouses. It now includes children. But—and it's a Big But—*we don't expect the kids to contribute to the common welfare to the extent that they are able.* Why is that?

According to Jennifer Senior in *All Joy and No Fun*, the role of children in the U.S. has been totally overhauled since the Second World War.[18] Whereas previously children had often worked and "kicked something back into the family till," in the modern family kids are protected from life's hardships. "Children stopped working," she says, "and parents worked twice as hard." Sociologist Viviana A. Zelizer put it this way, "Children have become economically worthless but emotionally priceless."[19]

The modern problem gets worse. Another sociologist, Annette Lareau, in *Unequal Childhoods: Class, Race, and Family Life* described another related parent-child phenomenon (especially in the middle class), which she called "concerted cultivation."[20] It's not just that the kids have stopped working and contributing. "Most aspects of the children's lives are subject to their mother's ongoing scrutiny" and parents face a never-ending series of scheduling and transportation duties involving soccer, baseball, gymnastics, chess club, computer camp, and so on.

This concerted cultivation, Lareau says, places "intense labor demands on already busy parents, exhausts children, and emphasizes the development of individualism" often at the expense of the family. Most of the burden, of course, falls on Manager Mom.

What are parents overlooking here? Two things. First, a setup like the one described in the last two paragraphs is a major violation of the Equal Suffering Law. Mom shops, does the laundry, cooks, cleans the kitchen, and then drives her twelve-year-old to soccer!? Even if Dad "helps out," the *child* here still falls into our ESL cheater category. Mom has no life of her own. Her daughters are likely to grow up to be overactive moms and her boys passive dads.

Second, we are missing the fact that children might actually want to not just "help out," but to actually do things themselves. What's the evidence? Exhibit A: Even toddlers want to do what big people do. In fact, preschoolers will often throw a tantrum if you don't let them help bake the cake or put the clothes in the washer. Now that's motivation! Exhibit B: Kids' self-esteem and pride are enhanced by being able to do things "all by themselves." Look at their inherent motivation, for example, to learn to crawl or walk. You did not create that drive. This leads to Exhibit C: Whether or not you cooperate, your children's long-term goal is to get rid of you! They want to be independently competent, do their own stuff, and manage their own affairs. That's the way it should be. Chronic parental supervision is bad—period.

As a matter of fact, there are some indigenous tribes in Mexico where children ages six to eight volunteer to do tasks such as cleaning the house, caring for younger siblings, helping prepare meals, and doing laundry. According to researchers at UC Santa Cruz, the kids want to do all this.[21] Young children want to do what the big people are doing. The authors also add that "the Mexican-American kids, aged 6–7, were doing about twice as much around the house as the middle-class European-American kids, on average."

How does the Manager Mom Syndrome affect our parenting culture? Here's the answer: *Manager Mom teaches children to wait until they feel they have to react to a parental command.* Manager Mom Syndrome does not teach kids to self-start. Why? Because everything is basically seen by everybody as Mom's responsibility. "Time to get up, Caitlin," "Eat your peas, Markie," "Don't tease your brother, Alyssa." But Caitlin is thirteen, Markie is ten, and Alyssa is eight. Can't they handle this stuff themselves?

As a matter of fact, just exactly what can children do on their own?

Executive Functioning

You hear a lot these days about what is called "executive functioning." Executive functioning involves *self-control*, and you might think of it as the ability to execute a plan. To execute a plan you have to do several things:

1. Remember the job: working memory

2. Remember the different steps required to complete the job
3. Carry out the steps without getting sidetracked

Toddlers, for example, are very distractible. Even tasks that take only a few minutes, such as brushing teeth, getting dressed, or going potty can be difficult for them to carry out. If these tasks are part of a larger sequence called "Getting up and out in the morning," toddlers may be lost. They forget what they're supposed to be doing, they get their sequences mixed up, and they get distracted playing with the dog.

As humans get older, though, they usually increase their ability to successfully carry out longer and more complex plans. This ability includes activities that they are not always particularly interested in doing. If we take homework as an example, here is a chart describing children's approximate capacities at different ages for doing independent school work:

Age Six: Ten minutes
Age Seven: Twenty minutes
Age Eight: Thirty minutes
Age Nine: Forty minutes[22]

If you have a seven-year-old in his bedroom doing homework, for instance, you might want to check him after twenty minutes to see if he's still on task. A nine-year-old, on the other hand, might last forty minutes with no adult direction or reminders. This list will give you some rough idea of what other kinds of activities kids might be able to carry off at different ages.

Now, think back to our big list of Household Tasks. Here it is:

Household Tasks

Cooking	Doing yard work	Making beds
Taking care of pets	Recycling	Cleaning bathrooms
Scheduling car maintenance	Watering plants	Managing money
Shopping (food, clothes, school supplies)	Doing dishes	Cleaning kitchen
Doing laundry	Dusting	Vacuuming
Straightening up	Cleaning bedrooms	
Scheduling activities (friends, family)	Taking out garbage	

Next, check out the executive-functioning capacity of a typical nine-year-old (see page 29), and what do you get? Hmmm...

Except maybe for maintaining the house or the car, a typically developing nine-year-old can do all that stuff, including the Household Heavy Hitters: food and drink preparation, interior cleaning, laundry, and kitchen cleanup. But we don't let them do it, and we don't train them to do it. We parents just prattle away in frustration about how busy we are, then drive the kids to soccer. Who does these household chores? Usually Manager Mom. Sometimes Dad.

There's more. What about our Childcare Basics list?

Childcare Basics

Supervision	Safety	Feeding
Hygiene	Potty training	Dressing
Grooming		

Same thing. A nine-year-old can do all that for themselves too. What about Child Discipline that involves positive behaviors?

Child Discipline

Adhering to bedtime	Doing homework	Getting up and out
Eating	Picking up	Sleeping though the night
Bathing	Brushing teeth	

What about negative behavior? A nine-year-old has the ability—if we train them properly—to control tantrums, arguing, whining, teasing, fighting, and other negative behaviors.

Same conclusion. A fourth grader has the potential to handle all this.

Children's Autonomy: The Bottom Line

So it appears we have a huge amount of untapped potential in our kids. Why is this? Four reasons come to mind.

First, we don't even think about asking our children to do meaningful household tasks, such as laundry, food prep, kitchen cleanup, shopping, or housecleaning. We think they shouldn't do these things because childhood is the time for us to enrich their lives, not burden them with drudgery. We forget that these tasks can be enjoyable for many people, and we also forget that *it's satisfying for humans to contribute to the common welfare.*

Second, we long ago gave up on the idea of asking the kids to make meaningful contributions because we don't feel we have a snowball's chance

We have a huge amount of untapped potential in our kids.

in hell of getting a positive response. Nagging, lecturing, and other parent prattle did not work, so we gave up. In just a bit we're going to talk about how to carry out meaningful responsibility transfers from Manager Mom to children (and also to dads!)

Third, the things we do tend to ask the kids to do are meaningless or silly activities that contribute little to the common good, like bake cookies, clean their rooms, or complete a weekend "chore list" involving trivial tasks.

Fourth, we convert tasks that kids can do on their own into primary childcare tasks in which parental presence and supervision are "required." It might be more accurate to say that—rather than converting these tasks into primary care—we never let go of them in the first place. We never systematically trained our children to be independently competent. Instead—with children who don't really need the help—we chronically supervise jobs like getting up and out, eating, dressing, homework, care of pets, and getting to bed.

Recall the executive-functioning skills of a typically developing nine-year-old.

By and large, parents enjoy seeing their children behaving independently and competently. Such behavior inspires affection and pride in adults. But more important than that, kids enjoy behaving that way! If we could find a way to get rid of Independence Deficit Disorder in our kids (to the extent that we are able), we could dramatically improve family bonding and decrease family ESL violations (get our kids out of the cheater category).

And Manager Mom might get another big chunk of her life back.

CHAPTER SUMMARY

Children have a tremendous desire to a) grow up and b) do what the big people are doing. This rule applies to toddlers, elementary age kids, tweens, and teens. In our culture, however, we do an absolutely awful job of tapping into and fostering this huge font of already existing energy!

FOUR

Your Maternal Identity:
The Ten Commandments

HOW DID WE GET HERE? How did Manager Mom Syndrome evolve in our family? We've seen how family bonding issues, the Equal Suffering Law, and children's Independence Deficit Disorder contribute to the Manager Mom Syndrome. But we've omitted one of the biggest underwriters of the condition. From the crucible of your growing up years, from your genes, from the culture you live in, and from the joy and tribulation of your becoming a mom, there arose inside your brain a rulebook for what it meant to be a mother. We call this your Maternal Identity, or Mommy ID. Your Mommy ID is perhaps the most powerful performer in the creation of Manager Mom.

Surprise, Surprise!

One mom I spoke with described this experience one school-day morning. It was a usual, hectic weekday morning at their house, with two parents, Brian and Karrie, trying to get two kids, Pierce (age seven) and Clara (age four) off to school. Pierce was having an unusually hard time getting his school bag organized, and Karrie was trying to help him but getting more and more frustrated by the minute. Meanwhile, Clara was running around in her underwear, hair a mess, and not anywhere near being ready to leave the house.

At this point, Karrie half yelled to Brian, who was watching the TV news, "How about giving me a hand this morning for a change? Will you *please* get your daughter ready for school—that means clothes and hair. I can't do everything."

Brian's response was a somewhat reluctant "OK, OK, no problem, I got it," and with that he picked up a giggling Clara and whisked her off to her bedroom. About ten minutes later, as Karrie and Pierce were heading out to the car, father and daughter emerged "ready" to go.

Karrie described to me what happened next. "I was stunned," she said. "Clara had on a polka dot top and striped pants with totally clashing colors. But that wasn't all. On her head, she had a pony tail, but not in the back. It was sticking up out of the one side of her head, more toward the front!"

Karrie went on. "Well, I couldn't let her go to school like that! People would think she didn't have any mother! What would the teachers think when they saw my daughter looking like that?"

"What did you do?" I asked.

"Well, I had to take her back into her bedroom and redo the

whole outfit—plus the hair part. I had asked my husband to help, but as it turned out, we were almost all late for school!"

I was intrigued with one aspect of the scene that hadn't been mentioned. "How did your daughter, Clara, feel about the outfit and look she and her Dad had come up with?"

Karrie hesitated for a moment, then she said, "She was thrilled with it." There was a distinct note of sadness in Mom's voice. She added, "You know, if I had to do it over again, I think I should have let her go to school the way she was. I disappointed my daughter, and I think I hurt my husband's feelings as well."

Final score: Mommy ID 5, Karrie 0.

Welcome to Your Mommy ID

All mothers have rules inside them for how their mothering activities should be carried out. These rules can be conscious, they can also be semi- or even unconscious, but they are your rules for how to play the mothering game. They are serious, and they are not to be violated. Your mothering rules can come from what you have read (magazines or books), from movies, from discussions with friends, from internet blogs, and, of course, from how maternal figures (moms, grandmothers, aunts, etc.) raised you.

Psychologists often refer to rules such as these as schema, mindsets, or core beliefs. These internal "ideas" can also include expectations about what mothering is or should be like, and what you can expect from kids and husbands. Maternal identity mindsets or schema often revolve around concepts like service, leadership, and first responderhood. They can also include attitudes about suffering, the legitimacy of meeting your own needs, about working outside the house, and about workloads inside the house. These mindsets can be healthy, they can be somewhat distorted (as in Manager Mom), or they can be horribly distorted (as in Martyr Mom).

Mommy ID Mindsets

The Mommy ID inside you is a rule book for being a good mother. It contains multiple guidelines for how *you think* a good mother should behave. Here's how the game works. If you feel you live up to a particular mothering guideline, you are allowed to feel good—but only for a few seconds. Then you are supposed to forget about your victory and get back to work. If you violate a rule, however, you are required to feel guilty for hours (and sometimes days), and you should also: 1) worry about repeating your offense and 2) engage in fruitless, circular obsessions about how to fix yourself.

Mommy ID rule violations, therefore, always carry with them a significant drop in self-esteem, which is usually very painful. Making modern matters worse, however, is the fact that these days we live in what I call a "fishbowl" type of existence. With devices like cell phones and apps like Facebook,

> *The Mommy ID inside you is a rule book for being a good mother. It contains multiple guidelines for how you think a good mother should behave.*

Instagram, Snapchat, Twitter, and more, it feels as though the whole world is watching *you*. It's like you're on stage. This fishbowl phenomenon has the effect of making your guilt, anxiety, and self-esteem drops feel much worse. And it makes the job of being a mother—and especially a Manager Mom—feel risky, fraught with emotional danger, and almost impossible to do well.

How does your family affect this situation? First of all, you worry about how your family sees you. Am I a good mom or wife in their eyes? Second, you feel that the "world's" judgments of you also depend upon how your family behaves—especially your children. And you can't always control what they do! Look up mommy blogs or read parenting magazines and you find frequent mention of moms feeling judged by others. It's like there's a contest going on out there to see who's the best mother.

Manager Mom's Ten Commandments

Here is a list of the top ten core beliefs or mindsets of Manager Mom. You'll see that these ideas all have a good or constructive component to them, but they each also have a significant unhealthy part. Add up all the unhealthy parts and you get the Manager Mom Syndrome. So—in addition to defining our greater goods—let's provide an assertive challenge to each of the ten mindsets or commandments:

1. *President*: A good mother is the president of the household. Kids and husband/partner are her staff. It is Mom's job to see that everybody—including her—does their daily jobs and chores well. That means Mom's way—immediately and correctly.

2. *Servant*: A good mom is also the chief household servant. Meeting her own needs must always come after seeing that the needs of her children and husband are met. Extreme self-sacrifice is just part of being a mother—that's the way it's always been throughout human history.

3. *First Responder*: If there is a problem at home or with the

family, Mom should always be the first one to respond to it, and she should remain involved until the issue is taken care of. Mom should also be in a state of constant preparedness for such unfortunate events.

4. *Stoic*: It makes no difference if mom is happy or not; she has a job to do. If Mom works outside the house in order to make herself happy, then she owes it to other family members to make up for the inconvenience to them caused by her not being around to provide childcare and take care of household chores like cooking.

5. *Competitor*: Most moms feel they should do their mothering better than most other moms. If they forgot to bake cupcakes for the bake sale and some other mom made two trays of beautiful chocolate brownies, they feel they should berate themselves and feel rotten. Moms feel they should always gauge what other mothers are doing and try to keep pace.

6. *Reflections:* Children are seen as big reflections on their mothers; it would be horrible if people thought ill of a mom because of how her kids looked or acted. She has to see to it that her children both look good and act good in public. Otherwise she will be extremely embarrassed and have a right to totally berate herself for carelessness.

7. *Dads vs. Moms*: Men care about their children a lot less than mothers do. Men are dangerous caretakers and can't be trusted with children, especially the little kids. Moms should always watch the little ones themselves. Dads tend to be selfish, preoccupied with trivia, and not attentive to childcare and household work.

8. *Mom's Work*: Whether she's working outside the home or not, tasks like childcare, laundry, food prep and cleanup, house-cleaning, and food shopping are the woman's job; these tasks should not be foisted onto others. Childhood is a time for carefree play. Mom should work to provide her kids with interesting and (even if expensive) enjoyable learning experiences.

9. *Vigilance:* The world is a dangerous place and moms need to be hypervigilant for any signs of danger to her kids. She should constantly worry and scan the physical, emotional, interpersonal, and psychological environments for signs of trouble. Mom should restrict her kids' activities whenever she senses the slightest hint of potential trouble.

10. *Free Time:* Mom's free time should always be spent with other family members. The ideal is whole-family fun. A mom who wants to spend time by herself is being selfish.

Well, there's a set of rules for you! If you're like most people, as you read the list you'll get uncomfortable—perhaps even anxious or irritable. You can feel the constructive, kind, and caring part of each item, but you can also sense an unwholesome, rigid, and anxious atmosphere pervading the list. When moms take each commandment to its extreme form, Manager Mom Syndrome rears its ugly head.

Mom's Rules for Others

Does Manager Mom have a rulebook for other family members? She definitely does. Like most members of the human race, Mom has a strong tendency to expect that other family members should think, feel, and act the same way she does. Dad, for example, should feel the same way she does about the kids, and he should act accordingly by worrying about their homework getting done and staying after them to get out of the house in the morning.

Mom has a strong tendency to expect that other family members should think, feel, and act the same way she does.

The kids should also be concerned about their homework, and they should care about keeping the house picked up and keeping their rooms clean. According to Mom, the children should offer to help with household chores and refrain from producing aggravating events like fighting with one another. Kids should have a sense of the common family welfare and how they can contribute to it.

In other words, mothers naturally expect kids and spouses or partners to facilitate their own efforts to carry out the Ten Commandments of the Mommy ID. The fact that others in the family do not, in fact, think and act that way is going to cause trouble.

Remember the scene that opened this chapter involving Karrie, her four-year-old daughter, Clara, and her husband, Brian? During all the fuss, what parts of Karrie's Mommy ID were operating? Answer: President, Servant, Competitor, Reflections, Dads vs. Moms, and Mom's Work.

CHAPTER SUMMARY

Each of our Manager Mom commandments is a mixed blessing. On the one hand, these rules motivate loving, caring, and sensitive behavior. On the other hand, however, these inner principles go way too far, and they and run the risk of crushing Mom's spirit.

FIVE

The Killer: Automatic Talking

B Y THIS POINT IN THIS book you probably have a number of ideas about what might need to be done to crush the Manager Mom Syndrome and get your life back. If you tried to proceed right now, however, the odds are 90 percent or greater that your efforts would be destroyed by an invisible—but highly audible—villain: automatic talking. Although auto-talk is a huge contributor to the Manager Mom Epidemic, it goes largely unnoticed.

Automatic Talking

It is often said that we parents are not trained for our jobs as moms and dads. That is certainly true. Policemen get trained, teachers get trained, plumbers get trained, and assembly-line workers get trained. You have to be trained to be a psychologist, a physician, and a physical therapist. You cannot drive a car without training and a license.

Why is training needed? Because without any instruction, when faced with a particular problem, human beings will still *try to do something*. There is a good possibility, however, that their action will simply be spontaneous, impulsive, and not tailored to the problem at hand. Their response might not only not solve the problem, but it might make things worse or even hurt somebody. In other words, in the absence of good training, an individual might *default* to an approach that is actually harmful.

That's what often does happen with parenting and with human communication. We are not trained in how to raise kids, and we are not trained in interpersonal problem-solving (see *Crucial Conversations: Tools for Talking When the Stakes Are High* by Kerry Patterson), so in a pinch we simply default to some behavior that is instinctive, natural, and sort of "feels right."[23] *This default behavior is often automatic talking, or what we call* auto-talk *for short*. When there's a problem, whether it's bedtime, homework, siblings fighting, or someone not carrying their load around the house, parents simply start to chatter, assuming this will make things better:

"This room is a mess!"

"What are you supposed to be doing?"

"Eat your cereal, then put your homework in your book bag."

"Why do I have to do everything around here!?"

Automatic talking is also known as prattle, babble, jabbering, and—guess what else?—nagging. (I asked before if you were tired of being the family nag.) Auto-talk is done not only by moms, but also by dads, kids, grandparents, teachers, presidents (of anything), football players, scientists, CEOs, and, well...anybody. Automatic talking is a huge part of the Manager Mom Syndrome.

"But how are you ever going to solve problems without talking?" a lot of people ask. As a matter of fact, people often assume that not only is talk necessary for solving problems, communication is simply great in general. The more communication the better, and even if talking does not help, it is at least a somewhat positive experience or at worst a neutral one. Right?

Nothing could be farther from the truth on both counts. Auto-talk is one of the main reasons—if not the main reason—human relationships are destroyed. It's a Big, Bad Human Habit. It often sounds like this:

"I asked you to feed the dog!"

"What did you do this time!?"

"Stop whining about every little thing—grow up."

"Drop that game and get moving!"

What's wrong with automatic talking? Two things:

1. Automatic talking irritates its listeners and consequently makes them *less* likely to cooperate.
2. Automatic talking interferes with kids' executive functioning.

Let's look at both of these bad effects.

Irritating Listeners and Decreasing Cooperation

Auto-talk (a.k.a. nagging) irritates people, and irritated people are less likely to cooperate with a nagger. Here's a good illustration.

Mom (Leona) walks by her daughter Brianna's bedroom. The room is a mess, and Brianna is lying on the bed with headphones on. Leona says, "What is this—this room is a mess! Come on, honey!" Mom starts this encounter with a verbal attempt to solve Brianna's messy room problem. Brianna's response to Mom's "What is this?" however, is, "Yeah, yeah. I'll take care of it."

Mom sincerely wants the room straightened. She was hoping Brianna would respond by saying, "Gee, thanks for the reminder. I almost forgot!" Yes, she would have loved that. Leona assumes talking is always a good thing.

Mom's question to Brianna reflects her inner wish to get a job done—but it only reflects her inner wish. And that's the problem with Manager Mom and automatic talking. Leona's initial question ignores huge, immediate, and obvious issues that involve another person's (her daughter's) thoughts, feelings and wishes. These issues are:

1. How will Brianna respond to Mom's question?
2. Will her question start a constructive problem-solving process?
3. What does her question say about who's responsible for Brianna's room?

We already know—with certainty—the answers to these questions:

1. Brianna will react poorly.
2. No constructive problem-solving will result.
3. Manager Mom is primarily responsible for her daughter's bedroom.

That's what automatic talking is: an impulsive statement that reflects the speaker's thoughts and feelings but which ignores the listener's thoughts and feelings as well as the probable outcomes of the conversation.

If you're a Mom here, you're probably mad at this point. You're thinking, "If she'd just clean it herself, I wouldn't have to say anything, for Pete's sake!!" True. But the real question is this: How do you get your daughter to that level of independence? Are spontaneous questions or suggestions getting the job done?

If you asked Leona and she took time to reflect, she would be painfully aware that her daughter never reacts in a positive way to that question about room cleaning. Never ever. She would know because she has asked the question hundreds of times. Then why does she keep asking? Because she's reacting only to her own thoughts and feelings. The thought is *What if she leaves her room a mess? That would be awful.* And so her consequent feeling is anxiety. Time to start talking! Leona does not really take time to think how Brianna is going to respond.

Brianna's predictable response, "Yeah, yeah. I'll take care of it," is her own version of auto-talk. The girl also defaults to mindless babble. But what's going on inside Brianna? She is irritated and she is immediately not in a cooperative mood. Brianna's thought is "I wish she'd shut up or go away." What she says reflects only that. Though this Mom-Daughter chatter is more mindless than malicious, it could get angry and vicious very quickly. No good "conversation" will result. No problem will be solved.

If your primary goal is to enjoy one another's company, even silence would be preferable to this angry and ridiculous exchange.

Auto-Talk vs. Kids' Executive Functioning

Our case against spontaneous parental chatter as a problem-solving device is pretty solid, and in Part II we'll discuss alternatives to this common Manager Mom difficulty. Believe it or not, though, there is yet another powerful reason why automatic talking is bad. A parent's automatic talking fosters Independence Deficit Disorder in youngsters by directly attacking kids' expanding executive-functioning skills. Adult chatter constantly reminds the children that their job is not so much to think for themselves as it is to quickly cooperate with a parental directive.

You'll recall that our description of executive functioning involved three basic functions:

1. Remember the job: working memory.
2. Remember the different steps required to complete the job.
3. Carry out the steps without getting sidetracked.

Executive functioning means doing all of these things *on your own.* If your children are going to break out of the prison of incompetence to ultimately get rid of you and live as independent adults, they must learn to manage lots of tasks, jobs, and problems by themselves.

But look at some of our examples of parental auto-talk and compare them to our three basic executive functions. What

do you see? You see that the adults' comments are replacing the children's executive functioning. "What are you supposed to be doing?" for example, replaces a child's use of their own *working memory*. "Eat your cereal, then put your homework in your book bag," replaces a child's perception of the required *sequence* of activities. "Stop playing with the cat" interferes with a child's learning to *focus* on the most important job at the moment rather than the cat.

In addition, constant reminders like these also carry a message:

"This room is a mess!"

"Eat your cereal, then put your homework in your book bag."

"I asked you to feed the dog!"

"What did you do this time!"

"Stop whining about every little thing—grow up."

"You know you only have ten minutes left on that game."

The volume, urgency, and repetition of these verbalizations say very clearly *"I'm still in charge here, and you're still incompetent."* That message is insulting to those hearing it, but you will recall that, by nature, automatic talking ignores listeners' reactions (insult, irritation) because the speaker is so focused on the intensity of her own feelings. Remember *Warriors and Worriers?* The key phrases were:

> *Freely*
>
> *Frequently*
>
> *Intensely*

So what do children, and sometimes dads, conclude as a result of the auto-talk barrage? They think this: "I don't have to worry (as in: use my own executive functions) about really being responsible for this homework, for eating dinner, or for going to bed or whatever. If trouble's coming, Mom will let me know way in advance!" "I'll wait for Manager Mom to wake me up. Who needs an alarm clock?" That's Independence Deficit Disorder.

Why Does Automatic Talking Persist?

Our discussion brings up a very interesting and important question: Why do parents repeat tactics, like auto-talk, that not only don't work well but that also make matters worse? Another way of asking the question is this: Why is it that rational, caring, and well-meaning human beings repeat over and over and over bad strategies—such as prattle and nagging—that result in frequent emotional suffering and lousy problem-solving?

In my forty years or so of working with families, this question has always intrigued me. We're not talking about nasty people here. We're talking about nice, intelligent, well-meaning people. Why do they keep doing (sometimes for years!) things that *always* make matters worse without doing much good? Why is there so often a total absence of creative strategy and friendly experimentation? I think I may have discovered a few reasons:

> *Why do parents repeat tactics, like auto-talk, that not only don't work well but that also make matters worse?*

1. In a half-baked, short-term sort of way, nagging works. Kids cooperate, but in a sloppy, unenthusiastic manner that teaches them nothing about self-starting.
2. Many parents also think, "We shouldn't need strategies. Kids should do what they're supposed to do and what they're

asked to do. I'll keep asking or commanding or nagging until they get the message. Kids should just behave!"

3. The default to reasoning and angry chatter happens automatically. Adults don't take the time to carefully think things over, and they're often feeling very *rushed*. "We've tried everything!" parents often tell me. Yes, but "We've tried everything!" usually refers only to reasoning, nagging, and yelling.

4. Lots of parents continue with useless and aggravating tactics because they simply don't know what else to do. They feel a sense of hopelessness. They don't really think there are other options.

5. Many parents are kind and have a deep desire to help. Is it possible to prattle and make things worse out of kindness? Yes it is. Strange but true, especially when a parent has no idea of what else to do.

6. Parents are angry. Anger makes humans very rigid and uncreative in their thinking. It's something like this: "If yelling doesn't work, I'll yell louder! If nagging doesn't work, I'll nag longer! Just put your foot down and be the boss!!" Often, thoughts like these do not involve well-conceived methods, they simply represent emotional retaliation.

We all want a warm and affectionate home, a reasonable distribution of labor, and self-sufficient kids. For those things to occur, we'll need to *transfer the responsibility* for a number of tasks and activities from Mom to other family members. But, as we've just seen, chronic supervision and auto-talk are not the way to get kids or dads to use their executive-functioning skills so that responsibilities really get handed over. If the simple repetition of commands were, in fact, a good method, it would have worked already. We need a new approach to relieve Manager Mom.

CHAPTER SUMMARY

Though family members don't always realize it consciously, the frequency, intensity, and duration of automatic maternal verbalizations send the message "I'm still in charge here and you're still incompetent!" to other family members. This is certainly not mom's intention! But the result is aggravation for mom and demoralization for fathers, partners, and kids. Ever had a boss who made you feel like you never did anything right?

SIX

Homework:
A Manager Mom Case Study

S O FAR WE'VE EXAMINED THE causes and side effects of the Manager Mom Syndrome in a more or less conceptual way. Now let's look at, in some detail, a flesh-and-blood version of Manager Mom in action so we can examine how the Syndrome affects everything and everybody in the house.

Here's a family of four: Mom (Marcia), Dad (Curt), eleven-year-old son (Max) and nine-year-old daughter (Alyssa). It's 6:30 p.m. and this group is finishing dinner. Marcia gets the ball rolling by asking Max an all-too-familiar question.

Marcia: Got any homework tonight?

Max: I suppose.

Marcia: What do you mean you suppose? You either do or you don't.

Max: How should I know?

Marcia: How should you know!? What!? It's your homework!!

Max: Homework is stupid. You know there's a lot of research by these big-wig guys that proves homework is stupid? All my teachers know that. It's useless.

Marcia: No, all your teachers don't know that or they wouldn't give you any work to do in the first place! Why do you have to give me such a hard time every single night? Homework reinforces what you learn in school. It's a good thing.

Max: No, it isn't! I saw this on TV once, too. They even had a middle-school teacher who admitted that homework doesn't do anything for improving achievement test scores. Now how dumb is that?

Alyssa: I'm going up to start my math.

Marcia: Thanks, honey.

Max: Oh, yes, yes! She's such an angel! Such a sweetie! Volunteers without even being asked. What a dear child!

Curt: Knock it off, buddy. There's no need for that attitude.

Marcia: Just get up there and get busy. You'll feel better when it's all over.

Max: Yeah, right. Death by a thousand cuts. I can hardly wait for the fun to begin. (Max slinks off to his room.)

Will Max get his homework done? Yes, but it will take two hours (about one hour longer than necessary) because he'll do it while he's angry, and he'll waste a lot of time. Now, if the bottom line—the primary parenting goal here—is *getting the work done*, the objective (homework completion) will have been accomplished. Max will have something to turn in in the morning and he won't get into trouble with his teacher. But how about getting the work done right, not to mention Max learning some independence and responsibility?

The primary objective—getting the work done—has been achieved by Manager Mom. But what were the costs regarding family affection, this boy's independence, and the fair distribution of labor around the house?

Family Affection and Bonding

We saw before that warm and friendly family relationships are everybody's goal, that these relationships powerfully reinforce both mental and physical health, and

Family bonding is a big deal!

that a reasonably happy home is a lot more pleasant and fun to live in. In other words, family bonding is a big deal!

Let's examine the Manager Mom role in our homework scene from this point of view. As far as family bonding went, the homework incident was pretty much a disaster. Who's going to want to come to the dinner table when this type of argument is likely to happen? No one.

And to make matters worse, consider this: You can think of a family as a group or you can divide the family into all of its possible pairs. Let's study what happened—as far as affection is concerned—to the different possible people pairs (or dyads) in our example.

Marcia and Max: The biggest conflict, obviously, occurred here between mother and son. Since this type of argument occurs on most school nights, these two will likely start dreading one another's company around this time of the day. Marcia may even start taking the long way home from work in the afternoon! Max may hide out somewhere in the house. At bedtime, Marcia's cursory "I love you" and kiss goodnight will do nothing to reassure her son, who will be thinking "You sure don't behave as though you love me!" In Gerald Patterson's *Mothers: The Unacknowledged Victims* terms, Marcia is an "Unacknowledged Victim" of the Manager Mom Syndrome. *Marcia and Max Summary: Major split. Now you know why some moms get depressed.*

Max and Curt: Less angry splitting than Mom and son, but still a fair amount of irritation. Curt doesn't like his son giving his mother a hard time, but he doesn't know what to do about it. Dad doesn't like to intervene unless Max is "getting too much of a mouth on him." *Max and Curt Summary: Mild to Moderate split.*

Curt and Marcia: These unpleasant times always make this husband and this wife irritated with each other. Though he feels she's right, Curt hates the sound of his wife's voice when she's nagging and arguing with the kids. He also feels Max is baiting his mother and that she's foolishly taking the bait! Marcia, on the other hand, feels Curt is unnecessarily passive and unhelpful. Why can't he back her up? *Curt and Marcia Summary: Moderate to Strong split.*

Max and Alyssa: This scenario is a sibling rivalry spat that Alyssa wins hands down. This girl is no dummy, and when her brother starts his dissertation, *On the Stupidity of Homework*, she sees a golden opportunity to score points by volunteering to go up and do *her* homework. Max knows exactly what his beloved sister is up to, and he feels compelled to retaliate by making fun of her. This move, however, further irritates Mom and brings Dad into the picture. Max knows a losing hand when he sees one and leaves. *Max and Alyssa Summary: Major split.*

Marcia and Alyssa: Interesting and complex. Mom is torn about how to react to Alyssa's offer to start her own homework. She knows it's a competitive, Goody-Two-shoes maneuver, but the girl is also cooperating and modeling positive behavior. *Marcia and Alyssa Summary: Mild bonding, but based in part on sharing a "common enemy," Max.*

Alyssa and Dad: Similar to Alyssa and Mom. Dad has mixed feelings about his daughter's behavior. He's glad she's cooperative, but he feels her timing here is almost vicious. Curt feels bad about Max getting a double put-down. *Alyssa and Dad Summary: Some bonding and some splitting.*

So in this scene, family bonding and pair bonding have both suffered a lot. Though the intensity of the anger could be worse, the frequency of these incidents (five times per week), their intensity, and their duration (often going on for hours) make them a major depressor of overall family spirits. Weekends provide a welcome break, though leftover resentments often carry over into Saturday. Everyone is sick and tired of the sound of the arguing and complaining voices—including the speakers themselves!

Why are kids tough on marital satisfaction? You just witnessed one answer to that question: homework civil wars. And that's only *one* behavioral issue. What if there are also problems (with Max and/or Alyssa) involving things like bedtime, whining, eating, tantrums, talking back, teasing, or getting up and out in the morning? More work and more hassles, primarily for Manager Mom, but also involving *everyone* in the family.

Max's Independence

The next question is this: What effects will this incident (and others like it) have on Max's independence? The answer is: very bad effects. Homework civil wars like this will teach Max several things: 1) homework sucks, 2) parental supervision sucks, and 3) "I would never dream of starting such a stupid and aggravating activity on my own." When Max does finish his homework, he will simply feel relieved that this obnoxious task is over for the evening. He will feel no sense of accomplishment. After all, why should he? *As it currently stands, his mother is the one who is responsible for his getting his homework done.*

I have found in my years of practice that repeated parent-child interactions like the one above not only help destroy personal initiative in children, but they also help create oppositional defiant disorder (ODD). This is the total opposite of being a self-starter and perhaps the essence of passive-aggressive behavior. With ODD personal initiative still exists, but it is often directed into more hostile and sinister directions. My opinion is that kids with ODD *enjoy* arguments like this, and they get *addicted* to them as a kind of entertainment or pastime.

Fortunately, the solution to the Manager Mom problem is one that will take homework responsibility away from Mom and put that obligation squarely where it belongs—right in Max's lap. Believe it or not, there is very likely a part of Max's brain that would like to do his homework—but totally on his own. We have to discover how to tap into that part. Manager Mom hovering over the family is not the way to get there.

The Equal Suffering Law

In Marcia's eyes, scenes like this one involve two clear violations of the Equal Suffering Law. First of all, Max is not doing *his* work—schoolwork. Marcia does her work—inside and outside the house. She naturally feels that Max should at least carry some of the load by doing his own homework. It would be nice for her not to have to worry about this task. But Max's homework has turned into a *primary childcare* task for Mom.

But there's another ESL violation. Marcia also feels Curt should "help" more. He could be much more supportive in trying to help her get their son to cooperate. Why doesn't he bring up homework at the dinner table himself instead of her having to always do it? Marcia feels that her husband is too often passive when it comes to the children. Issues like bedtime, getting up and out in the morning, sibling rivalry, and talking back come to mind for her. In these situations, she feels Curt should take the initiative—or at least back her up more aggressively. Too often—and in non-childrearing areas as well—Marcia feels she has to both identify a problem and then try to solve it on her own.

For his part, Curt feels his wife wastes too much time arguing with the kids. He is really tired of these arguments over this and that, and once they start he doesn't know if he's more angry with his kid or with his wife. What happened to that fun girl he used to date? Curt sometimes feels guilty that he is not more helpful, but when the children successfully bait their mother and a verbal spat follows, he thinks *Well, honey, you dug your own grave.*

The Manager Mom Syndrome does serious damage to family and pair bonding, it squashes kids' initiative, and it provides, in this family, another disruptive example of the Equal Suffering Law. Our case study illustrates several reasons why having children doubles the speed of the drop in marital satisfaction, why 40 percent of first marriages end in divorce, why women would rather do house-work than childcare, and why Dad golfs for five hours every Sunday morning.

How nice it would be (for everyone except Alyssa) if Max could do his homework on his own every night without being asked!

CHAPTER SUMMARY

The bad effects of the Manager Mom Syndrome:

- Family bonding/affection
- Equal Suffering Law
- Kids' independence

The daily goal of getting all the work, chores, and errands done—and getting them done right!—can blast family bonding, totally aggra-vate the Equal Suffering Law, and destroy kids' supposed-to-be-grow-ing independence. It's time for a Big Thoughtful Pause during which parents answer this question: What are our real daily and long-term goals for ourselves and for the family we are a part of?

PART II

HOW DO I GET MYSELF BACK?

Tools for Escaping Manager Mom

SEVEN

What Is Mom Doing Too Much Of?

I
F THE MANAGER MOM SYNDROME is an accidental family conspiracy in which all family members believe that Mom's initiative, guidance,
control, and follow-up are necessary for the successful completion of all
household activities, we should observe that, in fact, Mom is *doing more*
than other family members. We should see her not only worrying more
but working more than other people in the household.

Is this, in fact, the case?

What Is Mom Doing Too Much Of?

Believe it or not, to answer this important question the cavalry that is going to bail us out is none other than the United States Department of Labor Bureau of Labor Statistics. Every year this organization publishes something called the American Time Use Survey (ATUS). This survey tells all of us how—on average—we spend our time. It includes data on time spent sleeping, working, relaxing, eating and drinking, doing personal care, managing our households, shopping, and caring for children. These data are analyzed by age, sex, employment status, age of children in the household, and so on.

For our purposes here, the American Time Use Survey gives us good information on the average household distribution of labor (ESL) in the U.S., and it gives us some hints regarding the issue of kids' independence. The survey says nothing directly about family bonding.

Regarding the distribution of labor in U.S. families, we are interested in four parts of the survey:

1. Work outside the home
2. Primary care of children
3. Secondary care of children
4. Household activities

What will these data tell us about who's doing what at home and at work?

The Work Categories

Work Outside the Home. In the U.S. today, when a mother and father are both working outside the house, 47 percent of the time they are both working full time.[24] If we look at full-time work outside the home, the ATUS tells us that men averaged 8.4 hours per day (forty-two hours per week) and women 7.9 hours per day (39.5) hours per week. Women are more likely to work part time than men, however. When this is taken into account, if you average all working women and all working men, men average forty-nine minutes more per workday (about four hours per week) outside the house than women.

Primary childcare includes time spent providing physical care, such as dressing, bathing, playing with, or reading to children, assisting with homework, driving kids to events and attending those events, and taking care of kids' health problems. With primary childcare, a parent is *not doing anything else at that moment* other than that one activity with that child or children. Watching TV with a child, for example, is considered leisure, not childcare.

Primary childcare includes kids up to age seventeen, but the most difficult form of primary care involves children under age six. These are the ages when the kids are cute as buttons, energetic, careless, and a tremendous amount of work. This is the "high cost, high reward" time, and a steady diet of the little ones can be exhausting for adults. Tantrums start just before age two, kids stop napping around age three, bedtime and potty training become issues. But the smiles of these kids can light up the world.

According to the ATUS, on a typical weekday men spend 1.35 hours on primary childcare and women 2.81 hours with kids under age six. A lot of this activity (0.43 hours/day for men, 1.14 hours/day for women) involves the physical care of young children—feeding, bathing, and dressing. When both members of a couple are working outside the home, on weekends the man/woman difference moderates some: women are doing about forty-five minutes more than the men each day.

As the kids get older, the need for primary childcare drops considerably. Going from the under six category to the 6–17 category, men's primary care hours drop from 1.4 hours per day to 0.56, and women's from 2.65 to 1.07.

So the data tell us that when it comes to primary childcare, women are spending more time than men taking direct care of the kids. Keep in mind the research mentioned earlier showing that primary childcare was not a desirable activity for moms. It's not an especially popular activity with dads either, in spite of how loveable the kids can be. Primary childcare is an often fun but often exhausting activity. When both parents are working full-time, discrepancies in primary care hours become a big issue between moms and dads.

Secondary childcare involves children under age thirteen in an adult's care, but the parent or caregiver can be doing another primary activity. Secondary care is more like babysitting. The parent might, for example, be cooking dinner or talking to a friend on the phone while a child is at home. The ATUS assumes that, in general, kids over thirteen don't require constant supervision and it implies that these kids might be left home alone at times.

To get "credit" for these secondary care hours, however, parents have to be awake! According to the ATUS, being asleep doesn't count. It doesn't count if the kid's asleep, either. Hours count for secondary childcare from the time the first child under thirteen wakes in the morning until the last child under thirteen goes to bed. If a parent claimed on the survey simultaneous primary and secondary childcare, the activity is simply coded as primary childcare, not both.

The ATUS tells us that for the entire population, men average 4.22 hours per day (29.54 hours/week) and women 6.34 (44.38 hours/

week) in the secondary childcare of kids under age six. Interestingly, for kids ages 6–12 the guys' hours don't change that much, (4.04 hours/day, 28.28/week) and the gals' hours drop a bit (5.28/day, 36.96/week). That's because most parents don't leave children under twelve at home alone very much. For both sexes of parents, weekend secondary-care hours will average 2–3 hours more than weekdays.

In this secondary childcare category the moms still hold an edge in time spent, though not by as great a margin as occurred with primary childcare. The fact that a parent can be doing something else can make the time much less intense or stressful, but you still have to be home or with a child in case of emergencies.

Household Activities include activities done to maintain one's household and, as we saw before, provide for the common welfare. In general, men averaged 1.3 hours per day (9.1/week) doing household chores and women 2.4 hours per day (16.8 hours/week).

With what we call the Household Heavy Hitters—in terms of time spent—housecleaning, food prep and clean-up, laundry, and shopping, here are the data in hours per week:

	Men	Women
Housecleaning	1.75	6.79
Food Prep/Cleanup	2.94	7.14
Laundry	.58	1.98
Shopping	2.03	3.01

Men do more work in lawn and garden care (1.47 hours per week vs. .35 for women), and the area of household management (paperwork, money management) is fairly close between the sexes.

The Bottom Line?

So here's a summary of the hours/week data just presented:

	Men	Women
Full-Time Work	42	39.5
Primary Childcare		
Kids under 6	9.8	18.55
Kids 6-12	3.92	7.49
Secondary Childcare	29.54	44.38
Household Activities	9.1	16.8

Where both Mom and Dad work full time (now true in almost 50 percent of houses where both parents are employed), dads work about 2.5 hours per week longer than moms. In houses where both work but someone may work part time, dads work on average forty-nine minutes per day more than moms.

If you add it all up (which you can't quite do because of secondary childcare), you get the gals putting in more total hours per week than the guys do. One of the biggest strains, of course, is hours spent in primary childcare for children under age six, where the women put in almost an hour per day more. Kids over six are a lot less work, and in that area women put in one half hour more per day.

With secondary childcare, the kids under six again take up the most time and women spend more than two hours per day than men engaged in that activity. The mom/dad difference in time supervising children over six shrinks to an hour per day. Keep in mind, though, that with secondary childcare the adult can be doing another activity (such as housework or leisure) while more or less "babysitting."

For household activities, things balance out some in the areas of shopping, lawn and garden, and household management, but women still average about one hour per day more than men. This time is accounted for largely by the Household Heavy Hitters—interior cleaning, food/drink prep and cleanup, and laundry.

So, in general, women are working more hours at

A Manager Mom problem usually occurs where both parents are employed full time or close to it, and Mom puts in a disproportionate amount of the household and childcare labor at home.

home than men. Men work longer outside the house, but not enough to make up the difference. Keep in mind, however, that these figures are averages. In a situation where an employed father works twenty hours per week longer than an employed mother (e.g., forty hours vs. twenty), and the mother does 15–20 hours per week more than dad in household activities and primary childcare, a violation of the Equal Suffering Law may not be felt by Mom.

A Manager Mom problem usually occurs where both parents are employed full time or close to it, and Mom puts in a disproportionate amount of the household and childcare labor at home. The bottom line will vary some from home to home, and idiosyncratic interpretations of what is or is not a fair distribution of labor abound! But the result is often the same.

CHAPTER SUMMARY

Chronic fatigue and sleep deprivation are an enormous part of the Manager Mom Epidemic. It is a well-known fact that sleep deprivation causes accidents, distractibility, depression, physical health problems, irritability, and forgetfulness. The mother pictured here is this tired because other people in the family are not taking enough responsibility for their own lives as well as for their own families. This is going to change!

EIGHT

The ABCs of
Responsibility Transfers

IF MANAGER MOM IS DOING too much, it seems reasonable to conclude that there should be a switch of responsibility for various tasks from Mom to other family members. Those tasks being passed along will not involve work outside the house, obviously, but rather home-based operations like primary childcare, secondary childcare, and household activities and chores.

We will refer to these accountability handoffs as *responsibility transfers*. Someone is going to take over the obligation for certain jobs from someone else—in this case, from Mom. Since we now know *automatic talking is completely ineffective* in engineering such

If Manager Mom is doing too much, it seems reasonable to conclude that there should be a switch of responsibility for various tasks from Mom to other family members.

transfers, we are going to have to develop a new cognitive, behavioral, and emotionally based technology to effect these often difficult changes.

In this chapter, we'll focus more on the recipients of responsibility transfers: dads and kids. Won't they be surprised! What will be asked or required of them? How are they likely to respond? How will Manager Mom respond to their efforts?

In the next chapter, we'll discuss Mom's reactions to her own attempts to bring about change. Believe it or not, if kids and dads start altering their behavior in the direction you want, *you may not always greet their efforts with warm approval.* Your inner Maternal Identity, or Mommy ID, will want to have a word with you! You will often find yourself conflicted between The Old Way (where you were The Boss) and The New Way (where all these novices are slopping up your household).

If you are a Manager Mom, you are going to have to initiate the new changes. I guarantee you that your husband and children are not going to take that on themselves! It is not in their genetic makeup. You may resent Mother Nature for having created such a state of affairs, but that's the way it is. But keep in mind—and this will initially be a mixed blessing—your goal is to *assist in getting rid of yourself* in certain, well-defined aspects of primary childcare, secondary child-care, and household activities. Your goal is to get your life back by playing the game right.

When all is said and done, the ultimate objective of effective responsibility transfers is to enjoy the other people in your family, eradicate ESL violations, and help your children escape from Independence Deficit Disorder. It's also about your own mental health and about liberating healthy time for yourself. It's going to be a wild ride—brace yourself!

Total and Partial Responsibility Transfers

There are two kinds of responsibility transfers: partial and total. A total transfer of responsibility for a task from Person A (Mom) to Person B (Dad or kids) means two things—and both are extremely important. The first, obviously, is that Person B does the task from the moment of the handoff and on into the future. The switch is for good. The second criterion for a total transfer is this: Person A will not remind, prompt, or supervise Person B in order to get the job done.

Recall the model for executive functioning described earlier:

1. Remembering the job you're supposed to be doing.
2. Remembering the sequence of the subtasks required for the job.
3. Doing the subtasks in their proper order without distraction.

With a total responsibility transfer, Person B (often after proper training) does items 1–3 entirely on his or her own. Person A is not allowed to take over (via auto-talk) any of these executive functions from Person B.

In Chapter 13, Getting Up and Out in the Morning, you'll see a successful, real-life transfer of responsibility from Mom to her eleven-year-old daughter for the girl's getting off to school every day. Mom was allowed to say *nothing* during the actual training period as well as on subsequent mornings. The transfer was completed in four days.

Total transfers are usually preferable because they eliminate Manager Mom's emotional labor; but partial transfers, as you'll soon see, can also have their place, especially when it comes to training kids to handle certain household activities. Say you're training an eight-year-old to do food shopping. They can make the list and they can find the groceries, but they'll need your money and they can't drive themselves to the store.

What about transfers to Dad? In discussions about the fair distribution of labor around the house, the focus is usually on switching the work from Mom to Dad. Parenting magazines and Internet blogs constantly ask: "Do dads today really do more cleaning, bathing the baby, cooking or laundry than years ago?" As we have seen, the answer is "Yes." Dads *are* doing a lot more childcare and housework, though there's still a ways to go. But what we often find, however, is that these Mom-to-Dad responsibility transfers *are not total* ones. They are partial. Why? Because Mom still is reminding Dad to do the activity (executive functioning item 1 above), and sometimes supervising Dad's work (executive functioning items 2–3) while it is being done.

This is only a partial switchover of the accountability, and it is not that helpful for getting rid of Manager Mom. Why? Because Mom's mental load of worry remains the same. She cannot count on the work being done. She has to still think or worry about it—it's still "on her plate." Partial transfers have their place, but what we'll stress here is total transfers wherever possible. The more Mom engineers *complete* handovers, the more peace of mind she will achieve and the less emotional labor she will experience.

The same holds true with the children. Much of this success here will depend, of course, on the kids' executive-functioning capabilities at different ages. Mom will be much happier with total transfers, because the worry that motivates automatic talking and chronic supervision will be gone. And another family member—a child—will be much happier with themselves.

The Receivers of Responsibility: Dads

Theoretically, dads can take on tasks in any of the work categories mentioned before: primary childcare, secondary childcare, and household tasks (laundry, cooking, cleaning, etc.). Can a new father bathe a three-month-old without dropping them? Yes, he can. Can Dad "babysit" the three kids while you disappear on a Saturday afternoon? Certainly. Will your internal Mommy ID let you allow these events to happen? Hmmm.

You can think of dads as coming in three categories when it comes to dealing with Manager Mom and responsibility transfers. Here they are:

Cooperative Dads: "Ask and you shall receive." These dads are happy to help on one condition: *You have to ask at first.* Like any male of the species, they often are not sensitive to ESL problems. Even if they are, they usually won't bring the issue up themselves. Though the literature says they need reminders, you want to work toward *total* responsibility switches. You can bring it off if you play the game right.

Ambivalent Dads: These males are aware that you're both working full time and they may feel from time to time that the childcare/housework load is unbalanced at home, but they are torn between a desire to help and traditionalist views about sex roles. They are not interested in rocking the boat and getting stuck with more household work. Reminders and requests for "help" are irritating to them. You'll need firmness, you'll need diplomacy, and you'll need gentle but persistent follow-up. No chatter and no tantrums allowed.

Resistant Dads: Obviously, this is the toughest category. These guys don't see ESL problems to begin with, they wouldn't care much if they did, and your relationship with them doesn't provide you with much leverage in trying to alter the Manager Mom situation. You are not totally helpless, however, as you'll see in our later chapter on polite Guerilla Warfare. You can nicely exploit secondary child-care opportunities, make transfers to the kids, and terminate certain services on your own. You'll also be checking in and having some dialogues with your Mommy ID!

The Receivers of Responsibility: Kids

As mentioned earlier, most discussions of the fair distribution of household labor and the Equal Suffering Law involve moms vs. dads. The kids are left out. But, as we've seen, by age nine kids can do all kinds of stuff, like cook a four-course meal for their family and clean up after—not to mention shop for the food beforehand. Why don't they do just that? Because of *chronic supervision and automatic talking.*

Remember that children want to do what the big people are doing. Chronic supervision creates primary care where it shouldn't exist, especially where tasks like homework, getting up and out, fixing meals, getting dressed, cleaning up, going to bed, and personal grooming are concerned. We will address the problem of responsibility transfers to children shortly in many of our case examples. Often, kids are happy to help—if we let them and if we train them in a friendly, supportive, and patient manner.

We did our Dad categories based on Dad's potential

Often, kids are happy to help—if we let them and if we train them in a friendly, supportive, and patient manner.

willingness to cooperate. With the children we'll create approximate categories for them based on age:

Ages 0–5: This is a very taxing and crazy time for parents. The kids' executive functioning skills are close to zero! But what they do have is the desire to imitate adults, and they also like to please adults. The preschool years are the time when you want to tap into children's powerful, instinctive motivation to help out and emulate you. They may do a sloppy job and for a while it's more work than doing the job alone, but your allowing them to feel good about contributing and do some cool things (like run a vacuum, clean a toilet, or stir the pasta) will pay big dividends later. These initial training periods, obviously and sadly, will clash some with the Manager Mom goal of getting the work done *now* and getting it done *right!*

Ages 6–9: The executive-functioning skills of our first, second, and third graders (approximately) are growing quickly. That means that parents can proceed to more serious kinds of independence training—training that will often involve temporary use of partial responsibility transfers while on the way to complete handoffs. The kids can help with food and clothes shopping, help cook meals, start getting themselves to bed, perhaps do their own laundry, and do their homework more and more on their own. Though some kids will proceed faster than others, as Manager Mom *think of your goal as getting yourself out of the picture.* Don't use automatic talking and chronic supervision to keep your kids dependent on you. In other words, get out of the primary childcare business as fast as possible!

Tweens and Teens: Now the fun can really begin! You've probably always thought that kids can be really independent sometime around age eighteen or after they leave home. Wrong! You want your typically developing children *doing almost all their own stuff by age nine.* Sure, you'll still have house rules, hours, bedtimes, and some other general constraints, but you'll want your tweens and teens managing their own money, doing their own homework, getting up and out by themselves, doing some housecleaning, and doing their own laundry. You get the idea—and you get out of the picture.

If you are understanding the message so far, if you're a normal parent or a Manager Mom, rather than feeling elated about future possibilities, *you are probably feeling very nervous at this point.* That's because your Mommy ID is already starting to get after you, and your Maternal Identity is not a force to be taken lightly! If you don't understand, define, and learn to challenge your Mommy ID, you won't get anywhere when it comes to breaking the Manager Mom stranglehold.

So before we explore strategies and tools for escaping the Manager Mom Syndrome, we need to look at the monster within. Drastically reconstructing your Mommy ID will be your #1 Tool on the road to successful liberation.

CHAPTER SUMMARY

Responsibility Transfers in the Past:

- Mom to Dad: Partial ("Help")
- Mom to kids: Spotty or nonexistent
- Total responsibility transfers are rare

Good responsibility transfers and total responsibility transfers are tough—but not impossible—to bring about. They require the right kind of behavioral technology and a lot of self-restraint on the part of (a former) Manager Mom. But, once accomplished, genuine responsibility transfers are worth their weight in gold, and everyone winds up living in a much happier household!

NINE

Challenging Your Mommy ID

A T THIS POINT, YOU MAY have some reason for optimism. You perhaps have a vague idea of how you might carve out a new niche for yourself in your own family by using responsibility transfers. You also have a vague idea of how you might get back meaningful hours for yourself each week. And maybe—just maybe—these new hours will not be encumbered with interruptions, deadlines, or futile attempts to get other noncompliant humans to do your bidding. Won't that be nice?

Yes, it will, but you're not there yet. You will not get anywhere with your time liberation unless you are able to deal with the Ten Commandments that make up your Mommy ID. Your Maternal

Identity is going to have a lot to say about how far you are able to go with your emancipation. Your Maternal Identity is going to throw up obstacles to your success that range from the trivial to the sublime. Your Mommy ID is tricky, it is powerful, and *above all it wants to maintain the status quo.* This entity inside you believes ferociously that the way you are currently operating is the right way to behave. You didn't get where you are for no reason! Some of you will be able to deal with your identity-related stumbling blocks and create a new life, and some of you will sink beneath their weight and return to your old life.

Why Challenge Manager Mom Mindsets?

It's a fair bet that, overall, you are a reasonable and logical person. No, you are not perfect, and no, you do not do everything right, but you probably wouldn't be alive at all unless you basically attempted to live your life in a logical manner. You look both ways before crossing the street, for example; you try to do a good job at work, you eat pretty well, you sleep at night, and you get along with most people.

In other words, you have a fairly good rule book for living your life. You learned your rules from all kinds of people and in all kinds of places: parents, friends, movies, books, songs, teachers, magazines, houses of worship, doctors, and so on. But your life is not perfect, and sometimes things go wrong. Sometimes these things really bother you. "Things going wrong" can be due to two causes: 1) You have a good rule that you don't follow (e.g., A reasonable weight for me would be 125 and I weigh 150) or 2) You have a bad rule that you do follow (e.g., It is a terrible thing if I *ever* disappoint anyone, especially those close to me). Manager Mom involves the second kind of problem.

To deal with troublesome internal rules like these, many psychotherapists use an approach called *cognitive behavioral therapy,* or CBT. CBT takes the point of view that our upsets in life often come from irrational thoughts we have in certain situations. These screwy thoughts then produce emotional upset, which in turn produces maladaptive behavior. It goes something like this:

A. Situation

B. Thought

C. Emotional upset

D. Maladaptive behavior

Here's an example: Madison is flying from Chicago to Dallas to visit her sister who has just had serious surgery. Madison, however, has never liked flying. In fact, she hates flying. Here's how the A-B-C-D goes:

A. Madison sits down in the plane in seat 23A.

B. She thinks *This plane's going to crash during takeoff!*

C. Madison has an overwhelming feeling of nausea and panic.

D. Madison runs off the plane in tears.

If Madison went to a cognitive behavioral therapist, that doctor would first listen very carefully to Madison's description of her problem. Then the doctor would gently explain to this patient how CBT works. Next, this pair would confront the cognitive part of the problem, or Madison's B: "This plane's going to crash!" They'd ask if this is a reasonable idea and what are the actual chances that that would happen. They would together *challenge*, in other words, the illogical—or screwy—thought at B.

Madison's therapist would then turn her attention to the C part of the problem, the emotion. Madison would begin practicing strategies for relaxing, and she might pick her favorite from among meditation, yoga, progressive relaxation, deep breathing, or whatever. The doctor would then have Madison practice her breathing while imagining she's in an airplane flying to Dallas.

The next step? Madison's therapist would ask her how much it meant to her to see her sister in Dallas. Would she rather drive? If not, it would be time to consider making another plane reservation and using her new B-oriented and C-oriented tactics in the process. Simply put: Madison has a bad or erroneous thought that is preventing her from accomplishing something she really, really wants to do—visit her seriously ill sister in Dallas.

The As, Bs, Cs, and Ds of Manager Mom

The Manager Mom Syndrome is largely produced by the Mommy ID. The Mommy ID is a bunch of rules, thoughts, or mindsets that often produce significant emotional upset in Mom and, as a consequence, maladaptive maternal behavior. Using our A-B-C-D format, the process would look like this:

A. Household or family situation

B. Mommy ID Commandment

C. Strong emotion

D. Vigorous action

Imagine a mom, Alexa, and her eleven-year-old daughter, Willa, in the morning before school. Here's how the A-B-C-D sequence might go:

A. Willa is not dressed, and it's getting late.

B. Alexa thinks *It would be terrible if my daughter were late for school and it's my job to get her there on time.*

C. Alexa panics.

D. Alexa nags, yells, cajoles, and begs.

After several CBT sessions, Alexa transforms her A-B-C-D process into this:

A. Willa is not dressed, and it's getting late.

B. Alexa thinks *It's Willa's job to get herself to school. It will be unpleasant if she's late, but not terrible. It may take her a few days to take over responsibility for this up-and-out behavior.*

C. Alexa is nervous but in control of herself.

D. Alexa lets go and goes in the bathroom so she doesn't have to watch.

Notice that Mom challenged her Mommy ID successfully at point B in two ways. First, she convinced herself that her daughter's getting to school was really her daughter's responsibility and if Willa got there late it would not be an awful event. Second, Willa's lateness might be for the good, since it would help train her daughter to manage her own life.

Going back to our original example, with the help of her

therapist, Madison realized and persuaded herself that she wanted to see her sister *more* than she wanted to *avoid* a panic attack. She was going to Dallas even if she freaked out all the way down there—that was the greater good. Alexa did something similar. She wanted her daughter to become independent *more* than she wanted to *avoid* Willa's being late to school. Willa's autonomy was the greater good.

Four Greater Goods

Now we're ready to lay the foundation for challenging Manager Mom mindsets. To begin with, we're going to define Four Greater Goods that are more important than the Ten Mommy ID Commandments. Then we're also going to demonstrate what's illogical and dysfunctional about each of those ten rules.

1. *Mom's Mental Health:* The Manager Mom Syndrome makes mothers feel sick, unhappy, and resentful. That's no way to live. Do you think your family doesn't notice how you're doing? They notice all right. Taking care of yourself is critical for you and them—you can't separate the two.

2. *Family Bonding:* Time is slipping away. Each day your children get older and one more step closer to leaving home. It's time to stop this routine of seeing the kids each morning as a series of problems to be solved and time to start enjoying their company.

You have a right to expect children and dads or partners to take over (not "help with") childcare and household responsibilities to the extent they are able.

Think: Divide and conquer, ax unnecessary primary care, use responsibility transfers, etc.

3. *Equal Distribution of Labor:* You have a right to expect children and dads or partners to take over (not "help with") childcare and household responsibilities to the extent they are able. When they are ready, everyone contributes to the common family good, and—if you manage your auto-talk well—other family members will find their contributions satisfying. Think: Self-esteem—yours and theirs.

4. *Kids' Autonomy:* You don't want to raise helpless wimps. And you also don't want to raise children who simply respond cooperatively to parental commands. You want your offspring to self-start and think for themselves. If they're over age nine, for example, kids can cook, do their own laundry, get up and out by themselves, do their own homework, and help clean up the house. Think: patience, quality training, silence.

Attack! Challenging Your Mommy ID

Here is our list of the top ten core beliefs or mindsets of Manager Mom. You'll see that these ideas all have a good or constructive component to them, but they each also have a significant unhealthy part. Add up all the unhealthy parts and you get the Manager Mom Syndrome. So—in addition to defining our greater goods—let's provide an assertive challenge to each of the ten mindsets or commandments:

1. *President*: A good mother is the president of the household. Kids and husband/partner are her staff. It is Mom's job to see that everybody—including her—does their daily jobs and chores well. That means Mom's way—immediately and correctly.

Challenge: Mom does need to help organize daily activities, especially when the kids are little and have about zero executive skills. But Dad can be an organizer too. And we want the kids to take charge of self-care and household tasks as soon as they are able. Our priority is not mom's presidency, but competent independence for everyone ASAP.

2. *Primary Servant:* A good mom is also the chief household servant. Meeting her own needs must always come after seeing that the needs of her children and husband are met. Extreme self-sacrifice is just part of being a mother—that's the way it's always been throughout human history.

Challenge: Being a mother does involve a lot of self-sacrifice, but this sacrifice should not be extreme or constant. And Mom's activities should not involve doing other people's work. Mom should help train dads and kids to be autonomous. For their own good, dads and children also need to see Mom being happy, enjoying herself, and enjoying them.

3. *First Responder:* If there is a problem at home or with the family, Mom should always be the first one to respond to it, and she should remain involved until the issue is taken care of. Mom should also be in a state of constant preparedness for such unfortunate events.

Challenge: Mom needs to think and prioritize just what things need her intervention and what things other family

> **For their own good, dads and children need to see Mom being happy, enjoying herself, and enjoying them.**

members can handle. There are times when something bad happens when Mom should wait and give someone else a chance to respond. Waiting includes avoiding automatic talking!

4. *Stoic*: It makes no difference if Mom is happy or not; she has a job to do. If Mom works outside the house in order to make herself happy, then she owes it to other family members to make up for the inconvenience caused by her not being around to provide childcare and take care of household chores like cooking.

Challenge: Cruel and unusual punishment, this! Mom's happiness is very important to everyone. Mom's income is a blessing to all. And, finally, Mom's absence provides a special opportunity for other people to step up, take responsibility, become independent, and contribute to the common good.

5. *Competitor*: Most moms feel they should do their mothering better than most other moms. If they forgot to bake cupcakes for the bake sale and some other mom made two trays of beautiful chocolate brownies, they should berate themselves and feel rotten. Moms should always try to gauge what other mothers are doing and try to keep pace.

Challenge: Think hard! Am I really a slacker mom or am I taking care of business most of the time? Face it: Most moms are guilt freaks. Don't join that club! Plus, evaluations of other mothers are colored by the fact that most people put on their best face in public and hide their faults and weaknesses.

6. *Reflections*: Children are seen as big reflections on their mothers; it would be horrible if people thought ill of a mom because of how her kids looked or acted. She has to see to it that her children both look good and act good in public. Otherwise she will be extremely embarrassed and have a right to totally berate herself for her carelessness.

Challenge: Yes, children do reflect back on their mothers to some extent, but their behavior is also the product of many other influences, such as other family (kids and adults), genetics, teachers, movies, religion, TV, internet, and our culture in general. Within limits, you want your kids to learn to express themselves, and if that embarrasses you sometimes, so be it. Remember: No one else really has the time, interest, or energy to worry much about what you—or your kids—are doing.

7. *Dads vs. Moms*: Men care about their children a lot less than mothers do. Men are dangerous caretakers and can't be trusted with children, especially the smaller kids. Moms should always watch the little ones themselves. Dads tend to be selfish, preoccupied with trivia, and not attentive to childcare and household work.

Challenge: Of the two parents, moms usually do have a stronger bond with children for reasons already mentioned. But that does not mean Dad's love is weak or his caretaking sloppy. Dad's love is intense for his own kids and he will see to it that they are not endangered or hurt. Ironically, Dad is probably less attentive when Mom is nearby, since he tends to take a back seat to her presidential authority.

8. *Mom's Work*: Whether she's working outside the home or not, tasks like childcare, laundry, food prep and cleanup, housecleaning, and food shopping are the woman's job; these tasks should not be foisted onto others. Childhood is a time for carefree play. Mom should work to provide her kids with interesting and (even if expensive) enjoyable learning experiences.

Challenge: Whether Mom is working outside the home or not, it's reasonable to expect a fair division of labor for childcare and household tasks when everyone is together at home. Traditional definitions of men's vs. women's work when both spouses are working full-time don't apply anymore and need to be redefined. Kids need to pitch in when their executive skills make them capable of meaningful contributions.

9. *Vigilance:* The world is a dangerous place and Mom needs to be hypervigilant for any signs of danger to her kids. She should constantly worry and scan the physical, emotional, interpersonal, and psychological environments for signs of trouble. Mom should restrict her kids' activities whenever she senses the slightest hint of potential trouble.

Challenge: The world—and life itself—has dangerous spots in it, but it has way more amazing, wonderful, challenging, and enjoyable aspects to it. Too bad they don't include all that good stuff on the evening news! Moms can't lock their kids in the basement and they can't oversee all of their daily activities. Mothers have to train the children, encourage them, and—more and more—trust them to navigate their worlds well. Mom will have many nervous moments, and during some of those she will need to keep quiet!

10. *Free Time:* Mom's free time should always be spent with other family members. The ideal is whole-family fun. A mom who wants to spend time by herself is being selfish.

Challenge: Like anyone, Mom needs regular alone time for herself free of family. She also needs time during which she can enjoy one other family member for one-to-one relaxation and fun. Overdosing on family is a big mental-health mistake.

At this point, you can sense where we're headed, but perhaps you can't imagine yet exactly how we're going to get there. As we do our Case Studies in Time Liberation in just a bit, we'll continue to challenge Mommy ID core beliefs frequently. What is going to happen works like this. As you start to alter Manager Mom behavior, a Mommy ID mindset or core belief will attack you and try to stop you from changing what you're changing. You will need to know how to challenge your old mindset with a new and better (healthier for everybody) core belief before can you move on successfully. Takes a bit of practice, but it's a wonderful thing!

CHAPTER SUMMARY

Although your maternal identity mindsets are, in a sense, "only" ideas, they are tough customers. They can be sneaky, powerful, persistent, nasty, and persuasive! The chief tool they use against you is guilt, making you feel like you are being a bad mother when you ask or even allow other family members to take on new tasks. Don't listen to these culprits. You are entitled to more free time and a lot less emotional labor.

I am resigning as President, Servant and First Responder in the interest of family affection, kids' autonomy and a fair distribution of labor.

TEN

Mom's Declaration of Independence

YOUR MATERNAL ID IS A tough customer. It can make you rigid, angry, and judgmental. You can't approach other family members— the potential recipients of responsibility transfers—with that frame of mind if you want to be successful in enrolling them in your plan.

If you are a Manager Mom who wants to escape that role, before you try to do anything you need to take a look at your attitude toward the problem itself and toward the other people you live with at home. Below is a letter that you might want to use as a kind of template for either an initial written communication to family members or for a family meeting agenda. The letter says, nicely, that change is coming and it explains why change is needed. If you would like, run your customization of this letter by Dad or partner first, modify it so it reflects the interests of both parents, then present it to the kids.

Notice the tone of the letter is not primarily angry. There is frustration, but there is also understanding, gentleness, and a willingness to accept part of the responsibility for the existence of the Manager Mom Syndrome in your house. An angry, judgmental communication is worthless and destructive, and it will simply get you right back to where you already are. Oddly enough, you must remember that *you are never credible when you are tantruming.* You *are* credible when you are calm, decisive, and persistent. Calmness communicates to others that you really believe things need to change and that you are going to do something about it.

> *You are never credible when you are tantruming. You are credible when you are calm, decisive, and persistent.*

If you are a Manager Mom, reading this letter will also help continue your exploration of your Maternal Identity. While you read along, stop at points that make you angry, anxious, or uncomfortable. Discomfort will indicate issues that you need to think through before you try talking to anyone else.

Manager Mom's Declaration of Independence

Hi, Guys,

I've been thinking about some important issues that have to do with our family. First of all, we're not enjoying each other's company as much as we should. When we're together, it seems we're always rushing around trying to get some important errand or job done, or just trying to hurry somewhere in general. We ignore or bark at each other a lot at these times. Too much of the time I feel like the family nag and like I have to be in charge of everything.

That's no good. I want to enjoy you guys while you're still living with us! You'll be gone from home sooner than any of us realizes, and I want you and Dad and I to have mostly happy memories of these years. Those memories are not being created the way things are going now and that's got to change.

Second, I don't think Dad and I are allowing you kids to be as independent as you could be. This probably applies especially to me. It makes no sense, for example, if you are aged nine or older, that I should be trying to supervise your homework, get you up and out in the morning, do your laundry, and cook for you all the time. I could be wrong, but I believe you'd like to be more on your own and more independent as well.

I know what you might say here. You're going to say that if I'd keep quiet some of the time, you'd do all this stuff on your own. You know what? I think maybe you're right. Maybe—just maybe—we can test that out! You've already said as much to me on a few occasions, and I may actually take you up on your offer. My own opinion is that my talking so much in a "supervisory" capacity is understandably irritating to you and makes you less likely to take care of your own stuff.

So, how about we sit down sometime soon and make a few deals. We'll lay out what's going to be kids' responsibility and what's going to be Dad's responsibility and what's going to be Mom's responsibility around here from now on. Then I'm going to do my best to shut up.

Imagine, for example, that I totally left your homework from now on up to just you and your teacher. Imagine I said nothing about it—ever. No checking, no questions, no reminders. Maybe I just look at your report card. After all, it's not my homework! Wouldn't that be nice? Or would it? Would you ever get mad at me if, while I let you create your own successes, I also let you make your own mistakes? Do you think I could really bite my lip and not say anything about your homework in the first place?

While you're doing your homework and getting to bed on time by yourself (and doing your own laundry and maybe some of the cooking), I'm going to kick back, relax, and try to find some more leisure time. And I think I'll love you even more. That mutual affection might just go both ways, since hopefully you'll like my new, no-nag self more, too. We'll see. I think this could actually be fun for all of us.

When I was a little girl, I used to imagine being a mom and having kids. But I never imagined myself being a slave to my own family. Yikes! But that's the way it does feel sometimes. But let me be perfectly clear: I think this situation is partly my doing and partly your doing. It's a conspiracy between us! I talk too much, you pull back, do less, and wait for me to issue orders. I'm tired of being the family nag.

I want my life back, guys, and you'll enjoy my being quiet—I can guarantee it! I don't want to be the president around here. I do want to enjoy your company in the years we have left of your growing up in this house. I want us to have some real fun on a regular basis. Not just the family fun stuff, but regular one-on-one fun.

Can I suggest a starting place? Within the next month, I want to go out with each one of you for dinner and a movie. Sometime before we go out, I want to teach you how to do your own laundry. And soon after that, we'll address the distribution of the other household tasks around here: food and drink preparation, cleaning up the kitchen, shopping, etc. You can tell me what you'd like to do or not do. You know any good recipes you'd like to make for a family of four? Let's go for it.

Love,

Mom

Taking Stock

Before you continue reading, ask yourself four questions:

1. Take a moment and rate the *gravity* of your particular case of Manager Mom Syndrome: Is it Nonexistent, Mild, Moderate, or Severe?

2. Examine your own *automatic talking*. Does it come from anxiety, irritation, a desire to help, kindness, or some combination of those? Also look carefully: How do dads, partners, and kids react to your auto-talk?

3. How hard is it going to be for you to let go and let other

family members succeed or stumble on their own? What's your Mommy ID going to be telling you during this process?
4. What are you going to do with all your new free time?!

In the next chapter, you'll be examining more tools for carrying out responsibility transfers. Your efforts will begin with written, electronic, or verbal communications (letters or summit meetings) with other family members. Are you ready for these encounters?

Here's how you can tell if you're ready. If your attitude going into this project is "I want to get my life back by doing—gently and firmly—whatever it takes to enjoy my family, establish a fair distribution of labor around here, and help my children achieve maximum independence for their age," then you're ready. That's the attitude in the Declaration of Independence above. Go get 'em!

On the other hand, if your attitude going into this is "I want to convince my spouse or partner and kids that I am overworked, that they are underworked, that they are insensitive to my feelings, and that if they'd just step up and contribute around here without me having to do everything, all of us would be just fine!" then you're not ready. You won't get anywhere. Review the Declaration of Independence above again, reread the Mommy ID mindsets, talk to a friend, or better yet, find a good therapist before you tackle your family.

Time Is Short

Next time you're sitting at McDonald's having a hamburger and a Coke for lunch with your seven-year-old daughter and you're thinking about all the Manager Mom problems and worries you have on your plate for the rest of the day, consider this. Sure, you have things to do and you want to get your jobs done right. But right at this moment, there's magic in that hamburger, there's magic in that Coke, there's magic in your daughter, and there's magic inside you. If you just think to focus on it, the hamburger tastes good, the Coke tastes wonderful, and your little girl is really, really cute. There's shared one-on-one fun on your plate right at this moment. You don't want to miss it! At this moment in time, you like your daughter a lot and she feels the same way toward you. Priceless.

I have a friend from another state whose mother died recently. In a phone conversation not long after she passed away, I asked him if he missed her. His candid response was a bit of a shock to me. He said simply, "No, I don't miss her. You miss people you liked."

CHAPTER SUMMARY

Make your declaration, then back it up! It's time for action now, not words. Words will simply be more useless, aggravating auto-talk. Empty chatter or prattle will also convince other family members that you don't really believe in yourself and in what you are doing.

ELEVEN

More Tools for Responsibility Transfers

NOW YOU UNDERSTAND WHAT YOUR objectives are: Get rid of the Manager Mom Syndrome by establishing a fair distribution of work, increasing your children's autonomy, and strengthening personal affection in the family. Hopefully, your attitude toward this task is good—you are not resentful or judgmental, but rather open and flexible (and trying to be optimistic!).

You're interested in handing over responsibility for household tasks (laundry, cooking, shopping, cleaning, etc.), primary childcare (dressing, changing diapers, driving, supervising homework and bedtime, etc.), and secondary childcare. The recipients of your handoffs will be dads (or partners) and kids, whose capabilities will be determined in some cases by their attitudes (dads)—cooperative, ambivalent, or hostile—and in other cases by their ages (children).

It's time to start organizing your strategy—your approach for firing Manager Mom. We're going to use what we call a *time liberation model* to keep track of your progress. That means your efforts will be geared toward creating free time—time during which *you have a choice of what you would like to do.* You will no longer be completely locked in to Manager Mom tasks. You can call this free time, or mental health time, or Me Time, or whatever.

In executing your responsibility transfers, you'll want your attitude to be one of *friendly experimentation.* This means finding useful strategies for creating total responsibility transfers and for child discipline. Strategy identification means two things. First, you must identify the strategies you are currently using on a particular problem that are not working (the biggest culprit, of course, is automatic talking). Second, you must find new, more effective strategies for that same problem. In a friendly and open-minded way, you will then test these new tactics until the transfer is effected or the discipline problem solved. If one thing doesn't work, you'll try something else.

If one of your goals is your kids' (or your partner's) autonomy in carrying out, for example, a household task like cooking or cleaning, that means by definition that you are trying to *get rid of yourself for that task.* You'll find that is extremely difficult. Your Mommy ID will keep pushing to get you reinvolved. Why? So that things get done *now* and so they get done *right.* So that the status quo is protected! You'll want to do auto-talk. What happens if you do? Your chatter and your reinvolvement will squash any budding autonomy in anyone else.

In general, each time you seek to hand off responsibility, your campaign will have three parts: 1) a Kickoff Phase, 2) a Letting Go Phase, and 3) Careful Feedback Phase. You have certain tools you can use to help with each of these of parts of the change process. Let's look at the three phases and at your available tools.

The Kickoff Phase

To kick off the process of getting rid of Manager Mom and effectively transferring accountability, you can use the following tools: *Family or One-to-One Meetings, Quality Training,* and what I call *The Divide and Conquer Routine.*

Family or One-to-One Meetings: To discuss, agree upon, and explain new strategies, family or individual "summit" meetings will be essential for both kickoff and follow-up. These meetings can involve the entire family, or they can involve just you and one other person. These get-togethers define exactly what is going to be done differently in the home and by whom. It is often a good idea to write down what is agreed upon. You'll see many examples of Family or One-to-One meetings in the cases that follow in the next chapters.

Sometimes get-togethers to discuss changing the way people do things at your house can be handled in part by electronic means. Texts, emails, and even social media can be used to negotiate new arrangements as well as to provide positive or negative feedback about how things are going. Mom might tell Dad, for example, how much she liked her night out the previous evening. Or she might send a quick electronic message to her daughter about how good the meal was that the girl prepared the night before for the entire family.

If another family member is going to take over one of your jobs, often you (or someone) will need to train that person in that new skill.

Quality Training: If another family member is going to take over one of your jobs, often you (or someone) will need to train that person in that new skill. Some trainings, such as laundry, may take only two or three trials, while others, such as cooking different recipes and independent homework completion, may take a half dozen or so over several weeks or months (and some, such as social skills, will go on for years). Good training involves a good attitude on the part of the trainer-parent and good technique that is understanding, focused, gentle, and patient. Good technique is strong in positive reinforcement, calm and moderate in criticism, and accepting of mistakes and multiple trials. Anxious or angry auto-talk must be eliminated and put-downs are not allowed. Training, as we'll see later, also includes good child discipline methods for difficult behavior like tantrums, sibling rivalry, whining, arguing, and lying.

Training can be much tougher than you think. (I've done it, and I know!) Here are only a few reasons. Often, you'll find yourself wanting to explain how to do something that the other person already knows how to do. You'll want to talk and explain—and you'll irritate the other person and thus reduce their motivation to cooperate. Does Dad know how to use the washer and dryer, for example? Find out what he already knows first before you try to educate him.

At other times, you may have the impulse to explain something that the other person can figure out in less than thirty seconds if you leave them alone. Can your eight-year-old daughter, for example, flip a fried egg? Be quiet and let her fumble around, then reinforce her success with praise.

The Divide and Conquer Routine: One of the absolute best tools for accomplishing Manager Mom responsibility transfers is to use one-on-one situations—not whole-family times—to get the job done. *One* child with *one* parent enjoying *one* thing at *one* time is like emotional gold—it's extremely motivating and extremely useful. I call it the Divide and Conquer Routine.

Here's the deal: This will sound sacrilegious, but family fun is way overrated. Just like getting married and having kids doesn't always turn out as you might like, family dinners, outings, and vacations always have three inherent problems attached to them. Think about it. First of all, there are too many different opinions about what to do and how to do it. Second, with siblings aged three to seven, for example, fighting occurs—on average—three to four times per hour. And finally, kids *love having a parent to themselves*—with family "fun" this exclusive time doesn't happen.

In a one parent and one kid situation, you take away these three problems. What's left? A much simplified decision-making process about what to do, no sibling rivalry, and a child who cherishes the opportunity to have a parent to herself or himself. How nice is that!?

That is why Divide and Conquer is one of the absolute best ways to carry out good training, execution of a specific household task (cooking, cleaning, or shopping), or a two-person family summit. One-on-one fun is simply great for parent-child bonding, so it also helps the Manager Mom problem by enhancing mutual affection which, unlike automatic talking, *increases* kids' desire to cooperate.

KICKOFF PHASE

Here we go!

Family or One-on-One Summits:
"Here's the new deal!"

Quality Training:
Show 'em how it's done—nicely and patiently.

Divide and Conquer:
Tap into a motivational gold mine!

The Letting Go Phase

During the Kickoff Phase, you and one or more other people in the family defined and agreed to a new way of doing things. Manager Mom, for example, will be less active and less involved in some kind of primary childcare, secondary childcare, or household task.

During the Letting Go phase, the rubber meets the road. Your tools during this crucial phase will include *Natural Consequences, Silence, Challenging Your Maternal Identity, Sympathetic Listening,* and *Praise*.

The Letting Go Phase is time to put up or shut up. Actually, in a responsibility transfer it's *put up and shut up*! Someone else in the family now has to put up by doing something new, and Manager Mom has to keep quiet even when she feels something is going wrong. Mom and Dad *are* allowed, however, to offer—when necessary—spontaneous *praise* as well as support in the form of *sympathetic listening*. Corrective feedback will be reserved for emergencies, ex post facto family meetings, one-on-one get-togethers, and/or written and electronic communications.

Natural Consequences: With this tool, and with the kids especially, you are going to have to let the big, bad world teach them what's what and how to behave. Your job as a parent will be to get out of the middle (between your kids and the consequences), be supportive while the children are going through their transition-relearning period, and not engage in "I told you so's." The power of natural consequences comes from the child's direct contact with the effects of their own behavior, not with your (however brilliant!) explanation of the effects of their behavior.

The strategy of Natural Consequences can't be used for all behavior, and it works better for some things than others. You can't use this method, for example, to teach your kids not to run out in front of cars. Natural Consequences works great for getting to school on time in the morning, but not so well for getting to bed on time at night. The tactic can work well with lots of typically developing kids for homework completion, but not as well with special needs children for that same task.

When Natural Consequences works, however, it often works very well and its lessons sink in—without parental lectures. In fact, parental lectures can seriously impair the effects of this kind of "learning it the hard way." Moms and dads, therefore, have to know exactly what they're doing—as well as when to talk and when to keep quiet—when using this powerful approach.

Silence: Silence is a wonderful parenting tool! Listen carefully:

The Achilles' heel of all parenting strategies is their ignoring the need for parents to know when to keep quiet. As a mom or dad, you can ruin any good tactic by chattering on and by offering frequent prompts and reminders when they are not needed. As we have already seen, kids and husbands react strongly and badly to automatic talking. In the examples coming up, you will be presented with many situations in which keeping quiet is absolutely essential. Productive silence—combined with strategies like listening and praise—can assist tremendously with behavior from potty training to cleaning rooms to a child's cooking a meal for the entire family.

Challenging Your Maternal Identity: What are you going to be doing while—in the interests of an effective responsibility transfer—you're biting your lip keeping quiet? You're going to examine your own thoughts and feelings. The auto-talk we discussed earlier, which other family members often find so irritating, can be motivated by maternal anxiety and frustration, but, as we've seen, it can also be motivated by kindness and a desire to help. These are parts of your Maternal Identity or Mommy ID. The underlying motive, though, does not make automatic talking any less annoying.

Mommy ID > Automatic Talking! > Irritation in others

Sometimes sharing thoughts and feelings is a good idea, but during responsibility transfers often it is not. Responsibility transfers require moms to "let go" while dads and children learn new behaviors. During these transitions, even what seem to you to be kindly reminders from your Mommy ID can impede or even destroy progress. As you saw in Chapter 9, it is critical for you to be aware of what you are thinking and feeling on the inside. Why? Because your list of Mommy Shoulds often *need to be challenged* instead of being put into automatic chatter. Don't let inappropriate President, Servant, First Responder, or Competitor roles push you around.

Sympathetic Listening: So, no off-the-cuff reminders, criticism, or prompts during transfer times. This is really hard! What *can* you do instead? One tool you can use while things are in transition at home is good, sympathetic listening. As you'll soon see, your efforts to pull back will sometimes be met with everything from incredulity ("How can you do this to me!?") to pleasure ("Cooking is fun!") to confusion ("I don't know what to do!") to anger ("Dusting is dumb!"). You let everyone know you're serious not by becoming defensive, but rather by patiently watching and listening.

What is often called active—or sympathetic—listening is an excellent one-on-one bonding technique. It is also a great—or more accurately a *necessary*—prelude to discussing and resolving family issues, such as during a family meeting. You like and feel close to someone who listens carefully, respectfully, and thoughtfully to your opinions and feelings. You are a good listener when you are carefully trying to understand what another person is saying. You are a bad listener when, while they are talking, you are preparing your rebuttal. Sympathetic listening is good for learning how kids and spouses really feel about responsibility transfers.

Examples:

Family Reaction		Mom's Response
This is really weird!	⟶	I can understand that. It's strange for me too.
I can do this—fine.	⟶	You're on board, then?

I think this is dumb! ⟶ Explain to me why you feel that way.

Cool idea! How does ⟶ I don't know.
Dad like it? Why don't you ask him?

Statement	Sympathetic Response
"How can you do this to me?" ⟶	"It's hard on your own, isn't it?"
"Cooking is fun!" ⟶	"Looks like you're having a good time!"
"Now I know what to do!" ⟶	"You figured it out!"
"Dusting is dumb!" ⟶	"Don't I know it!"

THE LETTING GO PHASE

Natural Consequences

"This is hard!"

Silence

"But I have something important to say!"

Your Mommy ID

"Where did I get all these rules?"

Sympathetic Listening

"I need to know what they are really thinking."

The Thoughtful Feedback Phase

Many moms underestimate the powerful effects that their voices can have on kids and dads. After the Kickoff and during the Letting Go phases of responsibility transfers, you can have an impact on how well other family members cooperate or resist any new changes. Positive comments from you are

You can have an impact on how well other family members cooperate or resist any new changes.

OK, but criticisms or negative feedback have to be carefully managed.

Praise: In addition to good listening, another helpful tool you can employ is praise for initial efforts by dads and kids to do things on their own. As opposed to auto-talk—which is usually negative feedback—praise, or positive feedback, can be very useful in helping new behaviors sink in. Instead of trying to prompt or remind a child or husband to do something the right (i.e., your) way, you will learn how to keep quiet and wait for an opportunity to praise constructive, independent behavior. Be ready, because success won't always come in the shape or flavor you want!

For example, Dad said he would "make" dinner for the kids, ages four and six, while you disappear with a friend for four hours. What he comes up with is peanut butter and jelly sandwiches, black olives, and chocolate milk. You learn about this when you come home and your four-year-old greets you at the door with "Guess what Daddy made us for dinner?" What is your best response? Praise for both Dad and kids. Something like "I bet you guys enjoyed that! I certainly had a good dinner with Gail and the movie was excellent. Thanks."

Here's a bad response from your Mommy ID: "You call that a dinner!? If I'd have known, I wouldn't have left the house! From now on..." Ouch.

A fundamental and unfortunate law of human nature is this: Angry People Speak, Happy People Keep Quiet. Consequently, the effective use of praise is not easily accomplished. But praise will help your accountability handoffs—and your escape from Manager Mom Syndrome—a ton!

Careful with Negative Feedback! When you're giving positive feedback to Dad or children, there is usually no problem with the sound of your voice. Your message will be heard and probably appreciated. Negative feedback is trickier, though. The sound of a nagging, critical voice—combined with a negative message—can *obliterate the meaning of a communication.* The listener's reaction becomes all negative emotion, with no thoughtful appreciation of the corrective statement itself. "This room's a mess!" for example, triggers in a listener, either kid or Dad: 1) anger and 2) a thought such as "All you ever do is complain!" What you would like for them to think is "Uh-oh, my room is a pig sty!" and "I better get busy straightening it up!"

Careful feedback during responsibility transfers, therefore, can be done in several ways. The first is the normal—but sometimes dangerous—way of using the human voice (talking) during a summit or one-on-one (never give criticism off the cuff). A second tactic for negative feedback is via writing or stickers or numbers on some kind of physical, paper chart. Finally, a more "modern" way is by providing information on a person's task performance by means of electronic communications. Either can be done daily, weekly, or monthly. You can also get more creative by using emojis or other friendly graphics.

CHAPTER SUMMARY

Friendly experimentation: you're open-minded and flexible.

Now you also have a sense of what tools you'll need to accomplish your new goals. The hard part will be remaining silent while dads and kids stumble around and make mistakes as they engage in new behaviors. The fun part will be watching (affectionately) as dads and kids succeed in what they're doing and take pride in their newfound responsibilities. Yes, there is a training period, but you'll love the results!

PART III

INSTALLING A NEW REGIME

Case Studies in Time Liberation

TWELVE

Can a Seven-Year-Old Do His Own Laundry?

NOW LET'S START PUTTING INTO action our new tools for firing Manager Mom. And let's start having some fun! Sure, you'll have some difficult times in changing a behavioral pattern that has been persistent and one that involves the interaction of a number of people, but I guarantee you'll also enjoy the process.

We'll start with a household chore that takes a woman on average seventeen minutes per day, or about two hours per week.[25] This time is usually spent on the weekend, but it is also sometimes done on a weeknight after everyone else is in bed. The goal here is often to free up weekend time for more enjoyable activities.

The Task: Doing the family laundry.

Time Liberation Goal: One hour per week

Our Manager Mom in this instance is Sarah, and she's decided she should no longer be doing all the laundry for everybody in the house, which includes husband, Greg, and seven-year-old son, Noah. Sarah feels her husband is certainly capable of handling the job, though she doubts he wants to take it on. She also wants her son to learn the skill before he goes to college and before he gets married, so his future spouse won't have to go through what Sarah has gone through. Sarah admits feeling some resentment toward Greg over the years about his not doing *any* laundry *ever*, but she also realizes that she freely took on the job as soon as they moved in together without the two of them ever really discussing it. She was, in other words, a laundry First Responder.

Sarah and Greg have a good relationship, and Sarah feels her husband will be cooperative, though not necessarily enthusiastic.

So Sarah is going to engineer a *responsibility transfer* regarding laundry. Her objective will be to do this thoughtfully so that three important goals are recognized, respected and facilitated:

Family bonding: The new deal with laundry will reduce her resentment toward—and increase her affection for—Greg, make her proud of her son, Noah, for his new skill, and make Noah proud of himself. She also wants to set up the training so that Greg and Noah have some good times together. Her plan is this: She will train Greg (to the extent he needs it), and Greg will then train Noah. Greg will then do his wash, Noah will do his, and Mom will do only her own things.

Fair Labor Distribution: This violation of the Equal Suffering Law (involving both Greg and Noah not doing their share) will be eradicated. Why should she be doing their laundry?

Kid's Independence: Noah will be more autonomous regarding his self-care abilities. He'll be doing more and more by himself. Sarah thinks her husband and her son are both capable of running the washer and dryer, though she had to think this over a bit regarding her seven-year-old. But she eventually reasoned like this: If Noah can play some of the complex video games he does, he can run the washer and dryer.

The Kickoff Conversation

Sarah could use our Manager Mom Declaration of Independence, but she feels that might be more than what's needed. Yes, she's got the Manager Mom Syndrome, but her case is not severe or bitterly hostile. So she will use another tool, the *family meeting*, in which she'll first discuss her idea alone with Greg and get his thoughts. Sarah wants to avoid irritated automatic talking at all costs. So the couple makes an appointment to talk on Tuesday evening after supper. Since their relationship is pretty good, Sarah starts by saying, "I've been thinking of not doing everyone's laundry anymore. My hope is to get a little more free time during the week of maybe an hour or two."

Laundry Handoff

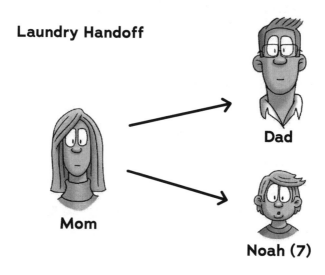

Mom

Dad

Noah (7)

Sarah's goal here is a *total* responsibility transfer of the laundry task to Greg and Noah—for their stuff, not hers. She offers to train Greg, if he needs it, and then asks Greg to train Noah. The ultimate goal would be for each person in the family to be doing their own laundry. Wouldn't that be nice?

Greg at first appears bewildered by—and then a little resistant to—Sarah's proposal. "Why can't she leave well enough alone?" he thinks. But after further review, he admits to feeling a little guilty sometimes that he's not been doing his own clothes and agrees to the proposal. Sarah is delighted with her husband's response. But Greg wants to take the deal a bit further. He will agree to do his own wash and to train Noah to do his own as well, but after the training period he wants his wife to stay out of it completely: no prompting, coaxing, questioning, reminders, or corrective comments. From then on, it's his job and Noah's—even if they destroy all their clothes.

Sarah hesitates, thinking, "But what if they mix whites with colors, or use the wrong spin cycle, or don't put in the fabric softener?" Being a basically logical person, however, she responds to these worries by telling herself that *those issues have to be dealt with in the initial training.* She also realizes, with some chagrin, that Greg's "no prompting, etc." comment was a reflection of his fatigue from and irritation with her automatic talking in the past. Well, at least now they share the same "no chatter" goal!

Ultimately, Greg and Sarah agree upon this definition for a total responsibility transfer for the laundry job:

1. Greg will do his own laundry from now on after being trained by Sarah.

2. Greg will train his son, Noah, to do Noah's own laundry from now on.

3. Sarah cannot issue reminders, prompts, or any kind of spontaneous corrective comments (automatic talking) because such talking would imply that she is still in charge of her husband's and her son's laundry.

4. Sarah can offer legitimate praise, sympathetic listening, or offer consultation or support *if it is requested.*

5. Sarah can offer any important corrective comments, but only at agreed-upon family meetings.

Training

Mom explains the washer, dryer, soap, and fabric softener to Dad. Then it's Greg and Noah's turn. Off they go! Greg and Noah take to the new task like ducks to water. It's a fun time for both of them, and Noah is excited to be able to push all the buttons on the washer and dryer. He also wants to experiment with these controls by doing the laundry in different ways (e.g., slow spin, cold water, normal heat vs. delicate). Greg lets his son experiment some, but they don't tell Mom about their research.

Over the following weeks, Greg lets Noah do more and more on his own—without any auto-talk from Dad! And pretty soon, Noah is starting and completing the entire task totally on his own. Greg is doing the same thing, and Mom is now—happily—worrying only about her own clothes. One week, in fact, when Greg is especially busy at work, he asks Noah to do both his own and Dad's laundry. Noah enjoys doing the extra work for his father.

Sarah guesses she has liberated one hour per week for herself, and she's starting to think about what other tasks she can hand off!

Letting Go and Sarah's Mommy ID

Sarah is somewhat surprised but also intrigued with her own reactions to the new laundry setup. The first time Dad and son do their laundry, Sarah's reactions are mixed. In addition to affection and pride, she is somewhat dismayed by the fact that she also feels a bit left out, a bit guilty, and a bit irritated. Her Mommy ID reminds her that laundry was supposed to be her job, and now these two "impostors" have taken it over. What makes them think they can do the job as well as she did? Will they fold the things properly? Will they use enough soap? She starts to say something (negative automatic talking) to the dynamic duo, but then she relaxes and restrains herself. Any necessary criticism or questioning can wait for the next family meeting. It's important for the two guys to get off to a good—and enthusiastic—start!

The second time she overhears Greg and Noah doing their wash, she feels very good. She feels affection for both of her "boys." Greg is actually doing housework, and she's delighted that Noah is also diving right in. The work is getting done, and it's getting done pretty well. Sarah's new mantra is Family Bonding—Fair Labor Distribution—Kids' Autonomy… Family Bonding—Fair Labor Distribution—Kids' Autonomy.

And Mom's mental health!

The Family Summit

In this chapter we got a glimpse of two of our Manager Mom Syndrome tools: the use of the family meeting and shared one-on-one fun. Let's take a closer look at both of these useful strategies.

Sarah chose to start the change process by meeting with Greg separately, and then talking to son, Noah, later. If she had wanted to, however, she probably could have met with both right from the beginning. For Greg and herself, she chose a non-busy, quiet time right after dinner. If a marital relationship is pretty good and a dad is cooperative, another good model is the date-night idea. If you choose this option, always do the meeting first and the fun afterwards.

I usually suggest not doing family meetings on a regular basis with children under five. These get-togethers take some self-control and a sense of what the objective of all the talking is: problem solving. Trying a family meeting, for example, with a three- and four-year-old is a good way to go insane inside of fifteen minutes. Also, consider limiting the meetings to an hour or less. Maybe it's just me, but these encounters can be tough, and going too long can just make a mess out of things. If things get heated, reschedule, then try again.

As the kids get older, you want them to have more and more of a say in the rules and policies that affect them. That's part of their growing independence, and as tweens and teens—whether you like it or not—your kids are already making more and more decisions without you, many of which you know nothing about.

Meetings don't have to formally follow Robert's Rules of Order, but they do need order of some kind. That includes an agenda, a chairperson (usually a parent, but can be a teen or even a younger child), respectfully taking turns, brainstorming, and agreeing on a proposal to experiment with. If Manager Mom called the meeting, for example, she might say "I'd like to put cooking and housecleaning on the agenda. What other items do people have?" Taking meeting notes is also a good idea. Family members—and especially quarreling siblings—often remember quite different things! A written record of what was agreed to will solve many disputes.

Family meetings can also be conducted with ambivalent or even hostile partners and kids. They can be done as a family group or one-on-one. If other individuals are not willing to sit down, one-way communication from Manager Mom ("This is how things are going to be from now on") via text, email, or simply in writing can get things started. Even if Dad or kids attend the meeting, sometimes they will not say much of anything. Too bad. In that case, calm, non-defensive, one-way communication from Mom is still better than nothing. Don't go off half-cocked in your mind about how you think others should or should not behave. State your case then keep quiet and *do* things differently.

Family meetings can feel a bit weird, especially in the beginning. But that weirdness also makes them memorable for everyone—and that unforgettable quality helps a lot. The fact that you're willing to do something strange says that you mean business and that things are going to be different!

The Divide and Conquer Routine

You'll almost always find that meetings with the whole family are harder to get through than are one-on-one meetings. That's because there are so many people in the room! This little piece of information gives us a hint about a basic psychological law of family life, which I like to call the Divide and Conquer Routine. As you recall, the Manager Mom Syndrome is partly based on a lack of family affection and bonding. The more affection you can find or produce in the family, the less stressed Mom will feel.

Here we run into a huge problem. How do you produce and strengthen the affection of family members for each other? If you ask adults in this country that question, you will always get the same answer: *family fun*. Sit everyone down at the dinner table, get everyone out to a good movie, take a family vacation. Sounds good, doesn't it?

If you really look at this notion, however, there are big problems. To whom does this whole-family solution look good? Mostly to Manager Mom. What about Dad? Dad has some doubts, but he suppresses those in deference to Mom. What about the kids? The kids would prefer to have one or both parents all to themselves. There are times when Dad would like to have Mom all to himself as well, and vice versa. These occasions are euphemistically called "date nights," but they are few and far between, especially when you have preschoolers.

Surprise: Pair Bonding Beats Whole-Family Fun

So what happens? Manager Mom, who is usually the Activities Director, engineers lots of family outings and other things for *everyone* to do. These activities can involve jobs, errands, and chores as well as fun. Sometimes, of course, there is no choice—everyone has to be together. The difficulty, though, is that *if affection and fun are the goals, one-on-one outings or activities beat whole-family activities by a mile.* Another way

> *Pair bonding produces much stronger affection than bonding that occurs when everyone is together.*

of saying this is that pair bonding produces much stronger affection than bonding that occurs when everyone is together.

We're going to mine this one-on-one gold to help get rid of Manager Mom. *Divide* up the family frequently in order to *conquer* the issue of family bonding and also to help with a whole bunch of other tasks, such as training, summits, household jobs, primary childcare, and kids' autonomy.

The power of shared one-on-one fun is amazing. In many situations, all you have to do to benefit from this new positive energy is *to think to do it*. Then relax and enjoy the benefits. But if this is really the case, why don't more moms and more families actually do the two-person thing? There are several very good reasons:

1. People—especially Manager Moms—just don't think of it.
2. Whole-family "fun" is seen as a powerful and worthy ideal. Whole-family activities are viewed as the default, or first choice, rather than events involving only two people. Family fun is what we're supposed to be doing, think moms and dads.
3. Moms, and sometimes dads, feel guilty when they deliberately leave someone out. "I'm taking John to the mall; Kara, next time will be your turn."
4. Kids can test and manipulate if they are the ones left out! Kara pouts because she's not going this time, and Mom feels bad.
5. Family fun is perceived as more efficient. We'll all go out to eat, then to a show. Our family-fun "obligation" will then be taken care of for the week.

In our laundry example, Mom cleverly set up the laundry training situation so father and son could enjoy one another's company, as well as *get the work done* and *get it done right*. Sarah had a feeling the two guys would have a good time and, sure enough, they did. Sarah's plan addressed another important issue with which we will end this chapter. The issue of father-child bonding. Why does Dad take so long in the bathroom reading the sports page? Why, in one video study of family interactions, was a dad in a room by himself the most common people/space configuration? If we can do something to foster father-child bonding, can we help erase the Manager Mom Syndrome? Yes.

Dad-Kid Bonding

You recall that one of Manager Mom's expectations for other family members was that these other people should feel about things the way she does. Dad, for example, should love the children as much as Mom does and be as responsive to the kids as she is. Is that really possible?

The answer in most cases· is no. Dad is a different evolutionary creature than Mom is and has had different experiences with the kids. Dad did not spend nine months with a growing baby inside him. When the baby arrived—even if he tried singing to the baby through Mom's stomach for the last five months of the pregnancy—Dad is still light years behind Mom in his attachment to the baby.

After the baby is born—contrary to what you may have read in popular magazines—things at home get tougher rather than better for everyone except the baby. Many new fathers feel the newcomer is a stranger. Even worse for dad, it's a stranger who just took away his best friend—his wife. Mom is now obsessed with the baby. Mom is also not herself—she's exhausted from frequent feedings and sleep deprivation. Dad might like to help out more, but he doesn't have the right equipment to feed the child, and Mom is very protective of the baby.

The result is that in many families, mother-child connection is stronger than the dad-child connection. So guess what happens? The Manager Mom Syndrome gets worse because mom gets stuck with more primary and secondary childcare (as we saw in Chapter 6). When there's a problem, the children tend to look first to Mom because that's what they've done since birth. And when there's a problem, Mom, as resident First Responder, reciprocates and takes care of the difficulty way more often than dad does.

Does Dad feel excluded or left out? Maybe a little, but not a lot. He's in the other room reading the sports page. He's not naturally a First Responder. In addition to making the Manager Mom Syndrome worse, though, Dad's natural inclinations also deprive him of something he hardly knows exists—the ability to have great fun with his own kids.

Dad-Child Bonding: A How-To Manual

If we can get dads more attached to their own kids, we'll help reduce the Manager Mom Syndrome. In addition, pretty much everyone agrees these days that it's a good thing for kids to be close to their fathers as well as their mothers. Fathers can be a very positive influence on their children. So how do you accomplish this?

Here's how you don't accomplish it: Whole-family fun. Whole-family fun is fine some of the time. The most powerful way to get dads involved with their children is the Divide and Conquer Routine: One dad and one child enjoying the same thing at the same time. Why does this work so well? The same reasons as before. There are only two people's agendas to coordinate, no sibling rivalry, and kids love having Dad to themselves. Family fun has its place, it can be a good thing, and often it's simply necessary. But it will never match one-on-one fun.

One-dad, one-child fun also provides two big bonuses, one for Mom and one for Dad. For Mom, when Dad takes responsibility for shared one-on-one time with a child, Mom's primary or secondary childcare burden is lessened. In fact, in two-child households Mom and Dad both now have one-adult-one-child opportunities for doing whatever and enjoying themselves.

What's the bonus for Dad? When Mom's out of the picture, Dad is running the two-person show. Dad will bond better and faster with each child if the outing is not under the direction of the local Activities Director. We often talk about kids liking autonomy, but parents like autonomy too! Dad will bond faster with his own children in situations where the whole family is not present. Period.

The list of activities dads can do with their own kids is very extensive and limited only by the creativity of Dad. Dads will also find that, once they get the hang of it, they can be exciting Activities Directors too! Why wait for Mom to come up with all the ideas? Dad and his ten-year-old son go to dinner and a show. Dad and sixteen-year-old daughter go to the gym to work out and then get coffee afterwards. Dad and seven-year-old son visit Grandma. Dad and eight-year-old daughter learn to cook pigs-in-a-blanket with baked beans and roasted brussels sprouts for everyone. Ten-year-old Doug and Dad vacuum and scrub the toilets on Saturday mornings, then go out for Italian beef—juicy with sweet pepper and fries. Sounds like fun!

CHAPTER SUMMARY

This chapter presents a fundamental lesson in how to get rid of Manager Mom. Switch the main goals from getting the work done now and getting it done right (my way!) to three more important goals: 1) a significant, genuine increase in family affection (in all directions!), 2) a tangible, meaningful, and more equitable change in the distribution of labor around the house, and 3) an important and worthwhile increase in a child's independence. Oh, and don't forget—more free time for Mom. Wonderful change!

THIRTEEN

Getting Up and Out in the Morning: Temporary Trauma

A S WE JUST SAW IN the last chapter, if you handle responsibility transfers from overloaded moms to other family members correctly, family affection will blossom, kids' autonomy will benefit, and perceived violations of the Equal Suffering Law will always be reduced.

So let's look at another example of responsibility transfer. You will soon appreciate that these handoffs come in different shapes, sizes, and flavors. The laundry switch in the last chapter was relatively easy. The one in this chapter will not be. This next handover involves a switch of the responsibility for getting up and out in the morning from a Manager Mom to an eleven-year-old girl. This case will include

> *If you handle responsibility transfers from overloaded moms to other family members correctly, family affection will blossom.*

training that is semi-traumatic for two family members, but—good news—fairly brief (only about four days).

Remember earlier I stated that we need to remove children from the "economically useless" category and put them back into the "economically useful" class. That doesn't mean the kids have to start making money (though when they're teens that's not a bad idea), but it does mean they need to handle their own responsibilities as soon as they are capable of doing so. Children doing what they are capable of doing takes an emotional and behavioral burden off parents—especially moms—because it eliminates unnecessary primary childcare. The kids, though, can still remain in the "emotionally precious" category!

Whatever group we put them in, with children we parents will find a powerful ally that our spur-of-the-moment, negative, sloppy, command-oriented approaches often ignore: Toddlers, tweens, and teens all want to *do what the big people are doing*. You'll see that in the case below.

A Bad Hair Day Every Day

This story involves a mother I worked with a number of years ago. Let's call her Alexa. Every single school day morning, Alexa experienced a harrowing up-and-off-to-school process with her slow-moving eleven-year-old daughter, Willa. Among the daily negative side effects of this process were the following:

Bonding: Alexa and Willa were always mad at one another, Alexa for her daughter's lack of cooperation and Willa for her mother's nagging; Dad was also irritated with both Alexa and Willa on a daily basis for the same reasons.

Children's Independence: Before our intervention, Willa's autonomy was being squashed. Mom was almost totally responsible for her daughter's getting to school on time, and everyone in the family knew it.

Fair Distribution of Labor: Willa was not carrying her load. Getting up and out to school should have been *her* job, not her mother's. Willa was eleven, plenty old enough to get up and out in the morning. Mom had an unnecessary added burden of stress, worry, and primary childcare.

Alexa generally thought of herself as a good mother, but she felt her "evil twin" emerged on school day mornings. Typical morning scenes involved things like Mom pounding on the bathroom door, yelling "Hurry up or you'll be late!" and threatening "If you're not out soon, no Xbox this evening!" In spite of all the theatrics, Willa experienced many close calls in getting to school and she was, in fact, late more than once a month on average.

Matters came to a head for Alexa when, at a parent-teacher conference, Mom and Dad were told by the teacher that elementary school children didn't come late to school, their parents made them late! The teacher added a long list of possible future, adult effects of early school tardiness, which included being fired from jobs for being late. After the conference, Alexa's husband stated that Willa's tardiness was not just bad for her, "It's bad for all of us. Our family starts every day totally stressed."

Family bonding, this child's independence, and fair distribution of labor, in other words, all went down the tubes every morning. Alexa decided enough was enough, but she was uncertain how to proceed.

Time for a Change

When I first spoke to Alexa, I could tell right away that she and her husband were ready to work. They both had had enough. So I outlined the plan. First, they were going to execute a transfer of the responsibility for getting to school from Mom to Willa. Using our friendly experimentation model, we would work on the problem until we got it right, and the new deal would commence with a family meeting. At that meeting Mom and Dad would explain an innovative plan to Willa in which she'd be responsible for getting herself up and out in the mornings.

While explaining the new procedure to Alexa, I added, "If I'm doing a good job of describing this new system to you, you should be feeling very nervous." She was. Her mind filled with "what if" thoughts. What if Willa overslept? What if she was two hours late? What if the whole new plan didn't work? Alexa's Mommy ID kicked in immediately with thoughts about acting like a bad mother and hurting or upsetting her daughter.

But Alexa was also a trooper. She and her husband met with their daughter and explained the new arrangement. They gave her a new alarm clock, set it for 7 a.m., and told Willa that would give her seventy-five minutes to get ready for school. From then on, everything would be up to the young girl and they would not nag her. In fact, they would say *nothing*.

Willa's reaction was predictable: She laughed hysterically, then said "Cool." Her *cool* was the equivalent of *whatever*. *Willa didn't believe her parents*. In particular, she thought, there was absolutely no way that her mother could ever deliberately let anything bad happen to her like being late for school. Mom would always save the day!

Fortunately, I had explained to Alexa that it was very likely that her daughter would be incredulous when she first heard the plan. So after Willa's "cool," Mom and Dad used their new tool: Silence. There was nothing else to say at that point. I'd seen many times before where the kids simply could not believe that their parents would actually shut up and let their own offspring face unpleasant consequences. Until it actually happened.

After the family summit, the next day was D-Day.

Up and Out Handoff

Therapeutic Shock

Willa was in for a surprise. The girl didn't know it yet, but she had a new mother! And today was going to be Willa's first day of boot-camp training. The girl's alarm went off at 7 a.m., and she slept right through it. Mom and Dad, of course, were both awake, and both were in agony thinking that her daughter might be late for school. To their credit, however, they stuck with the critical tool of Silence (in the face of extreme anxiety, irritation, and guilt), said nothing, and let their daughter sleep.

Mom also did a good job understanding the pushback from her own Maternal Identity. There was a war going on inside Alexa. Part of her Mommy ID said "You're a bad mom for letting your daughter get hurt by being late; what's the matter with you!" But another, newer chunk of her Maternal ID said "Your daughter needs to learn to get up on her own—she's eleven; good for you! Stay the course!" Fortunately, the second ID piece won the day.

Willa finally woke up at ten minutes to nine, a full twenty minutes *after school had started*! She wailed "I have a math test!" and started rushing to get ready. Mom and Dad remained silent but sympathetic. No "I told you so!" or "You didn't believe us, did you?!" as tempting as those comments might have been. Automatic talking would have ruined the lesson being learned.

Mom, however, was soon pushed to the breaking point by the sound of her daughter's shouting and crying. Her husband told her to lock herself in the bathroom and turn on the water to drown out the noise. She did. Dad drove Willa to school. Neither parent wrote a note of excuse. She sulked but did not cry, and then "marched with grim determination" into the school office.

I had assured Alexa that I had done this up-and-out training with families many times over the years, and that the cure (total responsibility transfer) usually took about 3–4 days. Sure enough, on the second day of the program, Willa used the snooze button three times, got out of bed at 7:30 a.m., accused her mother of being "a very, very mean mom," and then arrived (this time walking) to school ten minutes late.

On the third day Willa was on time and she continued to get to school on time after that. A few weeks later, Alexa reported that her daughter "had taken on new responsibilities and gained maturity." How was Alexa spending her mornings? Calmly sipping a cup of coffee and reading the paper. A huge amount of emotional labor had been eliminated. Nice job, Alexa.

The Mornings After

How did Willa's taking charge of herself in the morning affect the fundamental issues of family bonding, independence, and the Equal Suffering Law?

Bonding: When the training was over and Willa was done with her angry testing and manipulation, this family was closer. An hour or so of daily mom vs. daughter screaming, nagging, and arguing had been eliminated. So Mom and Willa bonded better afterwards. Also, Dad bonded better with Mom (and with Willa) because he didn't have to listen to all the ruckus. Finally, Dad and Mom were proud of their daughter's newfound independence. It was a major victory for family warmth and affection.

Willa's Independence: Willa had mastered a major life skill: How to get out of the house on time in the morning by herself. Setting the alarm, waking to the alarm, picking out clothes, dressing, getting breakfast, and making her lunch were now *all* her responsibility. Willa was aware of her accomplishment and proud of herself for being able to do it. *Kids want to do what the big people are doing.*

Equal Suffering Law: In the beginning, the main ESL violation here was not so much between husband and wife as it was between Willa and her mother. Mom was trying to do Willa's job. Sure, Dad could have joined Mom in the spontaneous-sloppy-naggy approach, but that would probably not have improved anything. As a matter of fact, Dad was very supportive of Mom during the process. This happy ending required not only the behavioral technology of how to effect a responsibility transfer, but it also included another important dimension: Alexa's taking her Mommy ID to task by changing—for the good of everyone—her internal rules for what it meant to be a good Mom.

Time Liberated: We'll give Alexa credit for retrieving an hour of time back for herself each weekday. That's five hours back each week. With the new regime on school day mornings, Mom could oversleep if she so desired, watch TV, exercise, or go to work early.

If Alexa and Sarah, from the last chapter, were actually the same person, that mother would now have freed up six hours per week from her Manager Mom bondage, one from laundry and five from converted primary care. Hmm, where else is there time to be reclaimed?

Your Firing Manager Mom Tools: Natural Consequences

The getting-up-and-out story we just described highlights two of the most useful tools you'll ever run across for firing Manager Mom: Natural Consequences and Silence. It's fair to say, in fact, that if you don't master these two tactics well, you will never escape the Manager Mom Syndrome at all. As you just saw, however, as beneficial as these strategies are, they are not easy to use. And they each depend on the other for success. Good use of natural consequences depends on your silence, and your silence, in turn, depends upon your ability to challenge your old Mommy ID and create a new one that serves both you and your family better. Let's look at Natural Consequences first.

Natural Consequences refers to a learning strategy where you let the big, bad world communicate directly with your child without you getting into the middle. Many people feel, as a matter of fact, that in helping kids master different skills, natural consequences is far superior to parental words and lectures. There are obvious limits to the notion, however, and many of these limits involve safety.

> *In helping kids master different skills, natural consequences is far superior to parental words and lectures.*

So in examining Natural Consequences as a useful strategy, we have to look at the skills we're trying to teach, the executive functioning abilities of the children involved, what might be the appropriate role of parents in this learning process, and, of course, the nature of the different consequences that might occur. Let's consider a few examples.

You have a nine-year-old daughter, Olivia. You're busy in the morning getting ready for work, so Olivia is supposed to make her own lunch and brown-bag it to school. You stock the cupboards with lunch bags and the fridge with other necessary ingredients. Out of the first four days of this new regime, however, Olivia has come home twice complaining "I was starving all day because I had nothing to eat for lunch!" What do you do?

Your Mommy ID, of course, hearing of your daughter's plight, will immediately throw out several "Good Mom" options to you. As a First Responder, you could take over responsibility for the problem. You could make Olivia's lunch for her, a great expression of the Servant role. Though this would increase your Manager Mom burden, Olivia might like this idea. In fact, some kids will whine or complain at you until you agree to do just exactly that.

Another option your Mommy ID might propose to you is automatic talking. In the morning you could remind (nag) your daughter about making her lunch or prattle on to her about how hungry she'll be if she doesn't. If she still doesn't cooperate, you could say "I told you so!" after school. As a respectable Manager Mom, this choice keeps you responsible for Olivia's lunch and provides no inspiration for her to become more independent.

Let's say, though, that your new Maternal Identity has convinced you that two things are necessary: 1) You want your daughter to start being more independent and 2) You want to escape the Manager Mom Syndrome. What are you going to do to serve those goals?

Just exactly this: Next time Olivia comes home and says "I was starving all day because I had nothing to eat for lunch!" you are going to say "I'm sure you'll do better tomorrow." That sympathetic listening comment is all you are allowed to say. Why? Because at age nine, Olivia certainly has the executive functioning skills to carry off this job and also because the consequences (hunger for half a day) are not lethal. If you let Olivia's tummy talk to her instead of her mommy talking to her, she will master the task in less than a week. I guarantee it. But she has to get burned a little to get the message.

Too many moms turn into guilt freaks while trying to walk through the Manager Mom Exit Door. "My poor baby will starve to death or get mad at me!" How do you deal with this guilt? Your "poor baby" is already nine, and she really needs to learn to be more on her own, and you (Mom) are entitled to more free time and more peace of mind. Those two things will come after a few initial days of "trauma."

Good Consequences and Not-So-Hot Consequences

The Natural Consequences strategy is a very interesting one to examine. Some consequences are therapeutic dynamite (in a good sense) for producing change, but other consequences are almost useless. Let's look, for example, at two problems: getting up and out in the morning and kids cleaning their rooms.

Getting Up and Out. For getting children age nine and over to school on time in the morning, Natural Consequences is a very effective tactic. Why? Because the consequences are so compelling. If a parent doesn't mess up the procedure with automatic talking (and also refuses to write a note of excuse), the child gets burned a little—nothing horrible or tragic. Willa, for example, had to march into school, explain to the office personnel, perhaps to the principal, and then to her teacher why *she* was late. All the rest of her class watched her come in tardy as well.

Because there are all these other people involved, Willa is legitimately embarrassed. That's good; that's appropriate. This awkwardness increases her *motivation not to go through this again.* Lectures or "I told you so's" from parents, on the other hand, *decrease her motivation* not to go through this again. The getting burned process is teaching Willa to be accountable for her own behavior. A total responsibility transfer is taking place. How nice for Willa and for Mom!

In addition, Willa's embarrassment occurs less than two hours after her mistake—not getting out of bed on time. The sooner a consequence (negative or positive) occurs after a behavior, the more effect it has on that behavior. This is good old-fashioned behavior modification, and in this situation it works well to help Willa learn.

Cleaning Rooms. What about natural consequences for kids not cleaning their bedrooms? Your fourteen-year-old son's room is a pig sty. You no longer remember what color the carpet is. The cat was last seen in there three weeks ago. Do you just let him live in the mess until he gets tired of it?

No dice. In this case, natural consequences won't work. It's obvious that having a messy room is of no or little consequence to your boy, and incremental increases in the mess have no effect. In other words, the first thing that happens to him when the mess gets worse is *nothing*.

So what do parents or Manager Moms do in situations like this? Too often, it's automatic talking, over and over. Auto-talk often escalates into arguing and yelling. What's the problem? The problem is that messiness for this kid has no major negative impact and other family members seeing the mess also has no major negative impact. It's very different from Willa's experience walking into school late! So this boy's parents need to think like this: "Well, we've tried natural consequences. No good. We've also tried nagging. No good. But he's basically a good kid. So, according to the principle of *friendly experimentation*, what can we do next?" See Chapter 14 for more about the central issue here: eradicating unnecessary primary childcare.

What are some other useful examples of constructive natural consequences? Got a child just starting piano lessons? Leave the practicing up to them and their teacher. You're not allowed to give reminders, but you can praise positive efforts. What about the wintertime dress of many tweens and teens? Is there a law for that bunch that forbids zipping up coats? Let them be a little colder but also a little more independent. Keep quiet and confront your Mommy ID.

Your Firing Manager Mom Tools: The Agony of Therapeutic Silence

In Willa's getting up and out to school case, her mother, Alexa, provided a graphic and wonderful demonstration of the agony of therapeutic Silence. Successful use of the Natural Consequences strategy absolutely depends on that ability to keep quiet at the right times. In Alexa's case that meant no waking her daughter, no reminding her to hurry up, no screaming, and no "I told you so."

For a devoted Manager Mom like this mother was, that self-restraint was a tall order to fill. But with the support of a cooperative husband, and the sound of running water to cover her daughter's wails, this Mom's silence allowed her stunned daughter to complete a total responsibility transfer—and to grow up a lot more.

With her own Maternal Identity screaming at her from inside "Bad Mom! Bad Mom!", Alexa was still able to successfully challenge those painful messages. In turn, she was replacing them with new messages that insisted on helping her daughter mature, become more autonomous, and become more of an adult. The new messages also included reassurance that her seemingly cold-hearted approach was actually necessary for family peace in the morning and necessary in order to ditch her commitment to unwarranted primary childcare.

Alexa's silence—and her sympathy for Willa's plight—also communicated two other messages to her daughter. First of all, her silence communicated to Willa the opposite of Manager Mom auto-talk. Instead of saying, basically, "I'm in charge here, and I'll direct this Morning Show because you can't manage it," her silence said "You, Willa, are in charge here from now on because you *are capable* of handling it. I wish you the best, and I'm proud of you for your new independence." That's good old-fashioned family bonding.

The second thing Mom's silence did was actually something that it did not do. Automatic talking by either parent would have (and for months had!) irritated Willa and made her less likely to cooperate. Silence freed Willa from the chains of anger paralysis and passive-aggressive behavior.

Firing Manager Mom Tools: Challenging the Mommy ID

Which of the Mommy ID Ten Commandments did Alexa need to face?

1. *President*: A good mother is the president of the household. Kids and husband/partner are her staff. It is Mom's job to see that everybody—including her—does their daily jobs and chores well. That means Mom's way, immediately and perfectly.

3. *First Responder:* If there is a problem at home or with the family, Mom should always be the first one to respond to it, and Mom should remain involved until the issue is taken care of.

6. *Reflections:* Mom's children are a big reflection on her. It would be horrible if people (like school personnel) thought ill of Mom because of how her kids looked or acted!

Alexa challenged these notions successfully. In the process, she became a new and better mom, and she also took better care of her husband and daughter. Though it was a real trial and a real trauma, this family came out a lot better after the turmoil. Natural Consequences, therapeutic Silence, and heavy-duty reevaluation of a Maternal ID all helped Alexa fire Manager Mom! Good!

CHAPTER SUMMARY

A tough—you might even say traumatic—lesson was learned in this chapter. But there's a wonderful ending! There are lots of applications for the basic lesson described here. Where would you like to start? Are you still asking your sixteen-year-old son about his homework or his clothes for school?

FOURTEEN

Eliminating Primary Childcare with Tweens and Teens

AT THIS POINT YOU'VE GOTTEN a feel for responsibility transfers to dads and kids, you know some of the do's (kickoff, follow-up, thoughtful feedback) and don'ts (automatic talking, yielding to Mommy ID threats), and you have some feel for how to do guerilla warfare when necessary (e.g., using secondary childcare hours, careful praise). You can now also imagine having more non-Manager Mom free time for yourself and, in addition, more peace of mind (someone else will do their job on their own)! That means less emotional labor.

In this chapter, we're going to retrieve more time for Mom by examining exactly what the *children* are doing and not doing. We'll refer to two lists of positive behaviors, which we'll call List A and List B.

List A. This list consists of constructive actions children can do that have two characteristics: 1) We expect kids to do these things sooner or later, and 2) The beneficiary of these activities is primarily the child. List A includes things like these:

Getting dressed	Personal hygiene
Getting up and out in the morning	Finishing homework
Going to bed	Staying in bed after bedtime
Caring for pets	Picking up your stuff
Cleaning your bedroom	Eating

What's the problem with List A? It's the "sooner or later" part. It's usually later! Nine-year-olds are capable of doing all these tasks, but we don't train kids to be independent and to do them. The result is nagging, arguing, unhappiness, lack of affection—in other words, chronic unnecessary supervision and lots of automatic chattering. In ATUS terms, these childhood milestones continue—daily—to fall into the category of *primary childcare,* and this childcare burden usually falls on Manager Mom.

It's no accident that the ATUS description of primary childcare explicitly includes "assistance with homework"! In addition, with average children around or over age nine, primary childcare from List A creates Mom vs. Dad ESL violations that would not occur if the kids were trained to do what they're capable of doing.

List B. List B consists also of constructive actions, but their characteristics are different: 1) We do not expect kids to do these things sooner or later, and 2) The focus of these activities is not primarily the child but rather the *common family welfare*. List B includes things like these:

Laundry

Shopping

Food prep and cleanup

Housecleaning

In ATUS terms, these are Household activities, "activities done by individuals to maintain their households." List B also contributes to an unfair distribution of labor between moms and dads because in our culture we don't want to burden our emotionally precious children with these chores. My philosophy, on the other hand, is that we should get the kids involved, not just with minor items like cleaning their rooms or taking out the garbage, but also with more useful and significant activities like laundry, cooking, shopping, and cleaning.

Truly independent and meaningful involvement by kids in the common good or family welfare will impact Manager Mom immensely, and it will raise kids' self-esteem.

Problems with Our List A Strategies

Why do we have such a problem with getting children to do List A behaviors on their own? The answer is straightforward: We don't think in terms of "what might be a good strategy for training?" Instead, we default to automatic talking and chronic supervision which, as we know, are usually useless and aggravating. Let's look again at our homework case study in Chapter 6 involving Marcia (Mom), Curt (Dad), eleven-year-old Max, and sister Alyssa.

Often we parents don't think of what we're doing with our children in a given situation as a *strategy*. We are more in the Just-Do-It-Dammit mode. On a Tuesday night, for example, your child probably has homework. That homework has to get done. So what do you do if you're the parent? Simple, you ask the kid if he has homework. If he tries to evade the subject, you nail him down. If, ultimately, the answer is yes he has homework, you tell him to do it. And then later, maybe, you check to make sure the work is finished properly.

Get it done now and get it done right. It's not rocket science— where's the need for a fancy "strategy," many parents ask? The job is simple and straightforward. That's what Marcia and Curt from our previous example were thinking.

Well, let's look at this line of reasoning for a minute. The question "Where's the need for a fancy 'strategy'?" is what's known as a rhetorical question. A rhetorical question is really a statement and not a question. The person who says "Where's the need for a fancy homework 'strategy'?" is really saying "There's no need for any homework strategy." If the kid has homework, you tell him to get it done. Kids should do what they're told, right? End of discussion.

Well, excuse me, Marcia and Curt, but you *are* using a strategy for homework—and it's not working! In fact, you're using several strategies. Furthermore, we can—if we just take the time to look—do the following: a) identify exactly what your strategies are and b) tell you exactly what's wrong with them.

What's Marcia and Curt's approach for getting Max to do his homework? The tactics of these parents (more of Marcia, of course, because Curt hangs back) involve several things:

1. These parents assume Max won't do his homework on his own. That's quite an assumption.

2. Mom, consequently, takes the responsibility for Max's homework by issuing what we call a "spontaneous request"—a comment that comes out of the blue. That comment is "Got any homework tonight?" Max, of course, balks as he always does and then tries to wriggle out of the noxious obligation.

3. When Max balks, Mom's next tactic follows automatically: angry reasoning. A really silly conversation ensues about whether or not teachers think homework is useful. Anger levels rise.

4. Meanwhile, what is Dad's strategy? Dad is passive initially. He doesn't get involved unless he thinks things are getting out of hand, which usually means that Max is getting a smart mouth and being disrespectful toward his mother.

5. Mom issues a command: just go upstairs and get it done.

6. When Max sees Mom and Dad both ganging up on him (and his sister making him look bad as well), he leaves the room and begrudgingly starts his homework, taking twice as long as necessary because his attitude toward homework stinks at this point. When Max leaves the dinner table, Mom and Dad say nothing.

So that is this couple's auto-talk-ridden, not-thought-out, basically lousy homework "solution": Assume Max won't do the work on his own, issue a spontaneous request, verbally combat "efforts to wriggle free," remain passive unless excessive disrespect occurs (Dad), issue more and more heated commands (Mom), and finally, remain silent as Max angrily complies (both parents).

What is wrong with Mom and Dad's homework strategy? After all, the homework gets done. If your primary parenting goal is only to complete daily chores, the conversation is over. But this couple's approach to homework also ruins family bonding, obliterates this kid's autonomy, and pretty seriously violates the Equal Suffering Law, causing more resentment between Mom and Dad.

Family Damage Prevention through Creative Brainstorming

Given the fact that family closeness is so important and everyone wants maximum warmth and affection at home, our nasty homework conflict repeating itself five times a week is surprising, but it is also tragic. You might think that after experiencing this routine for just a few days or weeks, Mom and Dad would start thinking: "This is awful! We have to do something *now* to stop this insanity! It would almost be better just to say nothing about homework at all, wouldn't it, rather than to experience this nonsense all the time? Homework completion isn't worth ruining a family!"

That kind of thinking would actually be a welcome start, but moms and dads often have to be nudged a bit to get to that point. They are stuck in anger paralysis. I've often said to couples who come in with parenting issues like this, "Well, the good news is that at least we know what doesn't work, don't we? We need new, different, and better strategies, because we've got a lot of work to do!" What's the work? Training the kids to *independently* perform all the items on List A and List B. Wow. Where do you start?

For practice, we'll start here by brainstorming Marcia and Curt's situation. Let's imagine that I have these two parents in my office. Let's also imagine that they now understand the notion of parenting strategy and, in addition, they understand the Manager Mom Syndrome and how anger has paralyzed and rigidified their past efforts. They also understand now that they *have to do something different* to save their family, help Max become independent, and provide a positive boost to their marriage. They simply have to.

What's the next step? I am going to brainstorm with them possible alternatives to the nightly homework situation. Any possible alternative option can be mentioned during this process, and in the beginning we do not criticize any new proposal. Brainstorming is an exercise in constructive creativity, not anger paralysis.

In doing our brainstorming, what question are we ultimately asking? The question really is "How do we find alternative tactics for helping Max do his homework on his own so that his homework doesn't stay in his mother's primary childcare category (no parental prompts, supervision, or correction)?"

Good question!

One way for us to start brainstorming is to take our original list of Curt and Marcia's six identified strategies and to try simply turning them on their heads:

1. Assume Max will do his homework on his own.
2. Consequently, no spontaneous requests from either Mom or Dad would be allowed.
3. Angry reasoning and silly conversations about the value of homework would disappear.
4. Dad wouldn't have to watch for disrespect.
5. Mom's issuing commands would be outlawed.

6. Mom and Dad might praise any positive homework-related efforts or comments that come from Max.

Many of you are now thinking: "So what, wise guy? What if he still doesn't do his homework? What if he still fails to complete his assignments?" Some would say: Go back to automatic talking! Surely nagging, spur-of-the-moment reminders, lectures, and other brilliant prattle will carry the day.

But you can't default to automatic talking again. How, in these complex modern times, do you find alternative tactics for helping kids do homework? Here are two good sources: *1-2-3 Magic: 3-Step Discipline for Calm, Effective, and Happy Parenting*, my bestselling childhood discipline book that has helped millions of families, and Google.

1-2-3 Magic, for example, has advice for *all of the List A behaviors* described earlier. Chapter 16, as a matter of fact, is entitled "Homework." There you'll read about the Positive-Negative-Positive Routine, the Rough Checkout, and how not to make spontaneous requests. You'll also read about using natural consequences for homework with kids over age nine. The Natural Consequences strategy is what Mom and Dad used with Willa in Chapter 13, you will recall, for getting up and out in the morning. Applied to this situation, Mom and Dad would say and do nothing (this should be the parents' new religion!), and let Max handle the issue by himself with his teacher.

Another place parents these days look for strategies is Google. Google something like "kids and homework," and you'll get a bazillion hits. Here are some ideas:

1. Have Max do the Googling and have him pick his favorite approach.

2. Go to NASPonline.org (National Association of School Psychologists' website) for advice.

3. Have Dad set up a homework routine with Max. This might help with independence *and* the Equal Suffering Law. Then, after a while, you have to get Dad out of the picture!

4. Set up a homework chart with artificial reinforcers. Max gets extra points for starting homework on his own without being reminded.

5. Ask the school counselor, Uncle Jim, or another trusted adult who isn't already involved in the daily family drama to act as a neutral third party and work out a homework routine with Max. No parental input allowed!

In terms of family warmth, Max's independence, and sharing the load, *anything's better* than what was going on in this family.

Hopefully, you get the idea. Old approaches like nagging and spontaneous requests have to be identified and then discarded. New discipline approaches, like parental silence, natural consequences, and charting, have to be discovered and then implemented correctly. Whether it's up and out, eating, bedtime, homework, getting dressed, or whatever, *we don't want List A stuff in Mom's primary childcare category*, especially when the kids are over nine. Many younger-than-nine children can complete these tasks as well.

Old approaches like nagging and spontaneous requests have to be identified and then discarded.

Lots of the tactics useful for List A tasks will also apply to List B (household) jobs. But List B stuff is different because it also involves more of a focus on responsibility transfers. In Chapter 16, we'll look at how to expedite responsibility transfers; then, in Chapter 17, we'll examine three household biggies: cooking, food shopping, and housecleaning.

CHAPTER SUMMARY

This question must be answered! Thoughtful, creative brainstorming is very difficult to do after Mom and Dad have already spent a long day at work and a child-related problem like homework, eating supper, sibling rivalry, or bedtime is staring them in the face. That's why lousy and spontaneous "solutions" like auto-talk are so hard to escape from. Consider doing your brainstorming on a Saturday or Sunday morning when your brain is fresh and rested!

FIFTEEN

Guerilla Warfare with Resistant Dads

WHEN DADS RESPOND TO A spouse or partner's attempt to improve family bonding, equalize the distribution of labor, or increase kids' independence, their reactions can vary quite a bit. As we saw earlier, their responses can fall into one of the following categories:

- **A.** Cooperative
- **B.** Ambivalent
- **C.** Hostile

Cooperative and Ambivalent Dads

With the cooperative group of fathers or partners, you will want to use the responsibility transfer procedures described earlier: agree on a new deal, let go and keep quiet, then follow-up thoughtfully. In our up-and-out example with Willa and her mother, Dad was a very cooperative dad. A lot of dads will be like this. Willa's dad totally agreed with the new regime (which he also helped initiate), and he provided much-needed emotional support and structure for his wife and daughter during the fairly traumatic training process.

Dads in the ambivalent category have decidedly mixed feelings about changes in household activities. They can appreciate their wives' points of view and see how the division of labor is uneven, but they are also set in their ways, and they don't like anyone rocking the boat. Like the cooperative dads, however, they value their relationships with their spouses or partners, and when they reflect on it, they do not want that person resenting them on a regular basis. So they are open to gentle-but-firm appeals to reason, slow-but-steady change, and consistent positive reinforcement for new behaviors.

In our laundry handover from Sarah to husband Greg and son Noah, Greg was initially an ambivalent dad. He was reluctant at first, not sure why the change was needed, and irritated by his wife's request. He was willing to go along with the transfer of responsibility, however, and—once they got started—he even enjoyed the work and his time with Noah. In other words, he was pleasantly surprised. *A lot of ambivalent fathers will react like this.* After his experience, Greg will very likely be more willing to take on other responsibilities, like cooking, shopping, and cleaning the kitchen.

So, with the cooperative group of dads or partners you might say that dealing with the Manager Mom Syndrome goes something like this: Ask and you shall receive. Why don't more women simply ask? Because their Mommy ID has not yet given them permission to make a pleasant, firm, and decisive request. Mom feels guilty about abandoning part of her Manager Mom role, the guilt makes her defensive and angry, and the "request" gets blown to smithereens.

Our ambivalent dads, however, present Manager Mom with somewhat tougher problems when it comes to modifying the status quo. But even though they don't see a need for change and they may not care so much about their relationship with their wife or partner, they still can respond positively to reasonable requests, slow change, and positive reinforcement.

What to Do with Resistant Partners

Sometimes parents still live together, but an emotional divorce has already taken place. The couple remains together due to two things: kids and finances. These relationships can take the form of constant subtle as well as outward hostility between spouses. These types of homes are very unpleasant places to live, they are hard on kids, and the Manager Mom Syndrome usually plays a large role in generating resentment. Hostile dads are more sex-role traditionalists. In their view, Dad works outside the home and Mom does the work inside the home—no matter what else she does outside.

What do you do with uncooperative, hostile partners? All is not lost, believe it or not. That's because you control a lot of the things you want to see changed, and your kids have some untapped power as well. Because of these two facts you can make a lot of headway—both on your own and with your children—in buying yourself back a decent life.

Imagine Aubrey and Oliver, who have been married fifteen years. They have two kids, Owen (twelve) and Courtney (eight), and their relationship now falls into the parallel-lives category. They don't hate each other and they don't fight a lot, but they don't particularly enjoy one another's company either. They are like ships pleasantly passing in the night. Mom and Dad both work full time; he averages forty hours per week and she averages thirty-seven. At home there are big division of labor differences that look like this regarding household tasks:

Hours Spent Per Week:

	Dad	Mom
Housecleaning	0	4.5
Food Prep/Cleanup	.5	8.0
Household Mgmt	1.5	.5
Shopping	.5	4.5
Laundry	0	2.25
Lawn/Garden	1.25	.5
Total	2.75	18.25

Aubrey cleans the house every couple of weeks—dusting, vacuuming, bathrooms, etc. She also food shops and prepares dinner every night as well as cleans up the kitchen. Oliver and the kids sometimes put their dishes in the dishwasher. Oliver spends more time managing the money, banking, looking at investments, and balancing the checkbook—about one hour per week. Aubrey does the laundry for everyone.

In regard to primary and secondary childcare, the chart looks like this:

Hours Spent Per Day:

	Dad	Mom
Primary	0.5	2.5
Secondary	3.5	4.5

Mom is the go-to person when it comes to primary childcare. The two kids seem to need daily supervision when it comes to getting up and out, they are often picky eaters, they don't do homework on their own, they have messy rooms, and they don't pick up after themselves in the rest of the house. Owen and Courtney also fight a lot with each other and appeal to Mom to be the arbiter. The kids fight less when Dad is around. However, in most ways they're just kids and they can be a lot of fun. Both parents like both children most of the time.

The New Regime

Aubrey wants her life back. The President, Servant, and First Responder thing is getting her down, and lately she's been more irritable. She realizes that her own Maternal ID, with the passive cooperation of husband and kids, has gotten her into a lifestyle where she's not really enjoying herself, especially since she's been working full-time.

In addition to not enjoying her own life, though, two other things are bugging Mom. She is not enjoying her own children as they rapidly grow up, and her kids are wimps—they are not learning how to take care of themselves and do things on their own.

Oliver is something of a "male/breadwinner and female/happy homemaker" traditionalist, and he's not going to change much. He's not sure he likes his wife working, though the money is nice. He's not a nasty guy or a jerk, that's just the way he is. In some areas, Oliver is about to find that he will have no choice but to do things differently. His wife is going to enjoy that, but she is not going to rub it in.

Where will Aubrey start? If her relationship were better with Oliver, she'd consider talking first with him. But in this situation she's simply going to write a brief note to all three of her bunkmates kindly and confidently stating the following:

Hi, everyone,

1. In our family we are not having enough fun together.
2. I am not having enough fun on my own.
3. This is going to change soon, but the changes are nothing you need to be afraid of. I am not leaving home!
4. I will answer any questions anyone has.
5. The new regime will begin in a week, starting with laundry and evening meals.

After reading Mom's note, the rest of the family has three reactions. They're a little nervous, they don't know what Mom's talking about, and they don't believe she's serious.

Starting Small But Strong

After the week is up, Mom provides Dad and kids with some real specifics. She's not going to bite off more than she (or they) can chew, but she's going to be like a rock in her resolve. And she's ready to deal with whatever protests her Mommy ID throws at her.

Aubrey's next move will be to write another note, but this time she will sit down at a family meeting to discuss the new deal. She can do this in a family meeting format with everyone all at once, or she can do it individually, whichever the kids and her husband prefer.

Mom's note says this:

OK, guys, here's what I'm proposing:

Two things: Cooking at night and laundry:

1. Evening meals: Three nights per week, I don't want to cook anymore. I will cook four nights a week. On the other three nights I'm suggesting this: One night Owen and I will take care of dinner; one night Courtney and I do the same. "Take care of dinner" will mean either cook or we go out by ourselves. If we go out by ourselves, whoever is left home is on their own. One night Dad will take care of dinner (cook or carry out). I'm looking for two things here. First, I want one night a week alone with each of you kids. Second, I want you guys to learn how to cook. You can suggest recipes or meals. A twelve-year-old, for example, is perfectly capable of cooking a meal for a family of four and an eight-year-old can start learning. And we'll have some fun during that learning process! We'll put a chart on the wall about who has what night.

2. Laundry: I'd like all of you to start doing your own laundry. You kids might enjoy learning how to use the washer and dryer, and it's something you're going to need to know how to do sooner or later. I think Dad already knows how to do it, but I'll consult with him if it's necessary. Dad or I can show you how to do laundry. This will

mean that—after any necessary training—everyone in the family will be doing his or her own laundry. Wow!

I suggest we start Monday. That's it for now. Let me know if you have any questions.

At any family meeting, Mom will want to put on her sympathetic listening hat. Anger or defensiveness from her will ruin her effort. She probably will encounter surprise, bewilderment, and sometimes irritation from her family, including possibly some of these reactions:

Family Reaction	Mom's Response
This is really weird! ⟶	I can understand that. It's strange for me too.
I can do this—fine. ⟶	You're on board, then?
I think this is dumb! ⟶	Explain to me why you feel that way.
Cool idea! How does Dad like it? ⟶	I don't know. Why don't you ask him?

No one likes sudden change. That's why Aubrey gave her family a week's warning.

Polite Guerilla Warfare

Even though Oliver is, on our rating scale, a hostile dad who is fairly resistant, he is still the kids' father, and he still can help his wife's efforts to fire Manager Mom—almost in spite of himself—if she plays her cards right. It's also possible Oliver will enjoy contributing more at home, even though he might not admit it. "Playing her cards right" means polite Guerilla Warfare, and there are useful tactics that can be employed. Mom's first guerilla tactic was to simply announce—very gently—what was going to be different and the specific services (already in her control) that *she was no longer going to provide* (laundry and some cooking). Aubrey's second guerilla tactic has to do with the interaction between the family meeting and the Equal Suffering Law.

The Family Meeting and the ESL. One good thing about family meetings is that they embody or express family values. One such value, for example, is to be kind to one another. Another is that everyone gets his turn to talk. At family meetings people *automatically think this is fair.*

Here's a good thing that will happen for you at your family meetings: The Equal Suffering Law will be in the room with you, and it will put pressure on Dad and kids to contribute more to the common welfare! Here's how that works. Both kids know who's doing and not doing what around the house, even though they may not comment on it. They also live in our modern culture, and they are old enough to be aware of and agree with the idea of a fair division of labor around the house. They've read

> **One good thing about family meetings is that they embody or express family values.**

about it, seen it on TV, or heard it at school. So has Dad.

Without anyone actually saying it then, three (or maybe all) of the four people at the meeting think that household tasks should be divided up more equally between Mom and Dad. Even though he doesn't like it, Dad will also be aware of that feeling in the family group. If Mom remains kind and sympathetic, Dad will realize that by doing supper once a week and doing his laundry, he will have a face-saving and relatively painless way to escape being seen as a cheater by other family members. If Mom gets guilty, then angry and defensive, however, Dad will use his reactionary anger to overwhelm his appreciation of the ESL. It's that simple.

Dad's Secondary Childcare Hours. Another guerilla strategy has to do with secondary childcare hours. Recall that secondary childcare is when a parent is home and there is a child under thirteen also home (and both are awake). The child is under the parent's care, but the parent can be doing other things. Now look at the table on page 158 for Mom's secondary childcare hours and Dad's. Dad has 3.5 hours per day, and Mom has 4.5.

Now hold that thought for a moment. Dad is home 3.5 hours each day while the kids are there. That means that Aubrey has *potentially 3.5 hours every day to leave the house.* She can do this, provided she can do one thing: trust Dad to be a reasonable supervisor while she's gone. The vast majority of dads, even those in the hostile category, have no interest in seeing their children hurt. If they know they're the only parent at home, they will rise to the occasion and do what needs to be done. It might not be exactly be what their partner thinks needs to be done, but it will certainly cover basic needs and emergencies. As a matter of fact, Dad is much more likely to handle matters better if Mom is not there! He will not, in other words, be in his reactive-resentful-passive mode.

Aubrey's Time Liberation. How much time did Aubrey free up here? Well, regarding laundry, she probably got back about an hour and a half per week. With regard to food prep and cleanup, she will retrieve about three to five hours per week, depending on what she does on her nights with each of the kids. It's either free time for Mom or good old-fashioned Divide and Conquer shared fun time.

What If?

What if Dad blows up the family meeting? What if he refuses to come? What if the child left at home to get his or her own dinner messes up the kitchen when Aubrey's out with the other one? What if Dad doesn't fold his socks (just kidding)? Lots of things can go wrong. Aubrey's feedback will be careful, controlled, delayed, and gentle—and very likely electronic or written. Initially, she is going to stick to controlling the behavior she can control—cooking and laundry.

We've discussed how to deal with difficult dads when you're trying to escape being a Manager Mom. The kids are another story. While Dad and kids may have some awareness that Dad is not holding his own around the house, the kids are not likely to see Independence Deficit Disorder as a problem for themselves even though it is. That's due, in part, to their ages and also to the fact that our culture doesn't expect much of kids. Other cultures—now and in the past—have had very different perceptions of children's responsibilities.

You realize that the ultimate goal of raising your children is for them to get rid of you and think for themselves, not for them to become good robots that respond instantly and agreeably to your demands or requests. They don't know it yet, but from you they're soon going to get some healthy independence training! In the next chapter we'll look at how to get more free time by transforming primary childcare into childhood independence.

TOOLS

PRAISE: HARDER AND TRICKIER THAN YOU THINK!

You're working your way out of a Manager Mom role, and other family members are cooperating by really accepting responsibility transfers. You have more peace of mind and more free time.

How are you going to react to this newfound wealth? Believe it or not, managing this pleasant situation is not as easy as you'd think. It certainly makes sense that you would want to recognize and praise other family members for their new contributions to your peace of mind and mental health. But nothing involving Manager Mom, it seems, ever comes easily. Even with cooperative dads and typically developing children, there's a hard part and a tricky part to using praise. And when difficult, traditionalist dads are involved, the hard part gets harder and the tricky part more complex.

PRAISE: THE HARD PART

On the surface, dishing out positive verbal reinforcement seems to be a fairly simple proposition. All you have to say at the proper moment is something like this:

> Thanks for doing the dishes.
> You got ready for school in record time this morning.
> Your room looks great!
> How did you know how to do that!?
> Got your homework done all by yourself again!
> I really like the meals you cook!
> That toilet you cleaned is sparkling!

So what's the problem? The problem is getting us adults to utter these words to begin with. Why? Because there's a universal part of human nature that goes like this: Angry People Speak, Happy People Keep Quiet. Unfortunately, this characteristic of humankind applies especially to families. If someone else in the family is doing something you like, for example, the chances are *you'll just enjoy whatever behavior it is and say nothing.*

If someone else in the family, however, is doing something that makes you irritated or angry, the chances that you'll say something to that person are much higher. Why? It's pretty simple, and it's partly biological. When you are

Angry People Speak, Happy People Keep Quiet.

content, adrenaline and other hormones are not flowing. You just sit and enjoy whatever is going on. When you're angry, however, adrenaline is released inside you, your muscles tense, you focus on what's bugging you, and within seconds you're ready for a fight.

Ten- to fifteen-year-olds, for example, have the highest rate of sibling rivalry. Imagine you're sitting watching TV with your eleven- and thirteen-year-old kids. They are not fighting. What are the chances you'll suddenly say "Gee, it's so nice to sit here with you guys and have a good time!" Answer: About 5 percent. What if the kids start arguing, then name-calling. What are the chances you'll burst out with "Knock it off, for Pete's sake, you're driving me nuts!" 95 percent.

So if you're a Manager Mom who is throwing off your chains and others are really helping out, just be aware of the Angry People Speak, Happy People Keep Quiet tendency. Do the best you can to toss out some positive verbal reinforcers, but accept the fact that it won't be easy for you. That's just the way we are.

PRAISE: THE TRICKY PART

To make matters worse, just uttering words of praise is only half the battle. The other part of the problem is this: Different people respond differently to different kinds of praise. Some people seem to like flowery, sugary, and effusive praise, but others seem to prefer more businesslike reinforcement.

Who likes flowery, sugary praise? Generally, small children. You can dish out effusive praise to three-year-olds, for example, for effort and performance that are really not very good (although their effort is usually pretty intense!). They will still enjoy the applause, though, and eagerly try to repeat their feat. Older kids, though, are starting to get wise to our adult tricks. Children seven, eight, and above are often able to appreciate how good their effort and actions really were, and they will become suspicious of overdone and inaccurate praise.

Then it seems there are some people who just like over-the-top praise and others who just like more unemotional recognition. When you're trying to reinforce dads or kids, for example, for doing household tasks, eliminating unnecessary primary childcare, doing necessary childcare, or whatever, you want to "tailor" your remarks to that person's preferences. It usually goes like this. You can give flowery *or* businesslike praise to a person who likes sugar with basically no harm done. For the businesslike kids or dads, though, unemotional praise is fine but *sugar will embarrass them,* and your praise will backfire.

Hostile, Traditionalist Fathers

These guys are tough to reinforce when they cooperate—actively or passively—with your efforts at liberation from the Manager Mom Syndrome. You also won't feel as much like praising them. I've found that when guys change in a positive direction, many former Manager

Moms—instead of feeling grateful—think something like "Well, it's about time you did your own laundry. Why didn't you think of that fifteen years ago when I started working!?"

That feeling on a mom's part is not perverse or vindictive, it's simply normal. Don't start kicking yourself around because you're not appreciative. That will come with time. Accept the reserve or grudge inside yourself and do the best you can to be appreciative to the extent that you are able. Believe it or not, there's good news in these situations. You don't have to worry so much about making the overly sugary, flowery mistake. Why? Because you won't feel much like dishing out syrupy-sweet acclaim in the first place, and these guys wouldn't like it if you did.

Any praise to hostile, traditionalist males, in general, should be brief and subdued but also genuine. That's because these male-female interactions can become quite delicate and awkward. Here's an example: Whitney comes home at 11 p.m. on a Saturday night after going out to dinner and a movie with a friend. Husband Michael agreed—very begrudgingly—to stay home, feed, entertain, and then put the two- and four-year old to bed. This is something he had never done before.

Whitney comes in glowing—she had a great time. Michael is in a sullen, martyr-like mood. Each senses immediately and understands the other's emotional state. Whitney goes sugar:

"Oh, we had such a good time! I can't thank you enough for staying home and watching the kids. It really meant a lot to me."

A good job of positive reinforcement, right? Wrong. Whitney unwittingly just cut her own throat. Her emotions were genuine, and she had felt free again. But Michael is going to interpret her message in a different way. He hears this:

"I hope you're not too mad at me. Maybe I shouldn't have gone out and left you. I know the kids are really my job."

Michael has her where he wants her. He's aware of his wife's Mommy ID. He grumbles something unintelligible, but his manner clearly shows that he did not appreciate what just happened and does not want it repeated.

Unfortunately for Whitney, Michael's interpretation of her praise for him was mostly correct! She is afraid of his disapproval, and in some ways she does feel she did the wrong thing, and she *is less* likely to do it again. She did not analyze her Mommy ID and challenge it, so her husband could challenge her face to face and win the battle.

The alternative? Whitney walks in the door and challenges her internal rules: "It's great for me to go out. Michael does need to share more in childcare, which can be rough with preschoolers. He'll have to deal with not liking it. Fair is fair around here."

What does she then say? A simple and matter of fact "I had a great time. Thanks."

CHAPTER SUMMARY

Polite Guerilla Warfare

- You control your own behavior.
- The current division of labor is unreasonable.
- You have a right to terminate unreasonable behavior.
- Very good for kids to contribute to the common welfare to the extent they are able.

SIXTEEN

Expediting Responsibility Transfers

A T THIS POINT YOU CAN appreciate the benefit of getting out of the primary childcare business. This strategy gives you more free time, makes you proud of your children, makes the kids proud of themselves, and helps the kids achieve greater autonomy. The tactic also gets Dad more *into* the primary childcare business, especially when the kids are little.

What if you started thinking something like this: "I really like this new way of doing things. How can I speed up the process? How can I get my kids and husband to do even more and get the distribution of labor around here even more reasonable?"

Good question, and there is an answer to it. The first thing you must do, of course, is squash the ever-present rumblings of your Mommy ID. Your Maternal Identity will tell you you're being selfish and abandoning both the kids and your responsibilities. You respond to your inner critic by reminding yourself that your kids have a right to—and a need for—independence, and you have a right to good mental health. You also want to equal up the childcare responsibilities between you and your partner or spouse so you can feel more loving and appreciative of that person.

How can you speed up this whole process? You have at least a couple of options: 1) Vigorous Independence Training and 2) Getting Out of Dodge. Let's look at each one of these freedom-producing possibilities.

Vigorous Independence Training (V.I.T.)

Some kids will take to the independence thing like birds to the air. Once they get a taste of the freedom and satisfaction they feel from doing things on their own, they are thrilled with what they have accomplished and want to do more. They are still kids, of course,

> *Some kids will take to the independence thing like birds to the air.*

and still benefit from your praise and approval, but that approval is now coming from their *autonomy* rather than from their *willingness to follow your directions.*

Let's say you just successfully trained your daughter, Kylie, to do her own laundry. Kylie is eight and a half. Now she tromps proudly downstairs on Saturday afternoons—without your prompting—carrying her own blue laundry basket. Next she turns on the washer, clicks the appropriate settings, separates whites from colors, puts in the soap and clothes, and she's off to the races. She likes to run the dryer on Delicate and she never forgets the fabric softener. You walk by occasionally to drop off a smile and appreciative comment.

For the laundry transfer, you followed the Kickoff, Silence (Let Go), Non-Verbal Feedback, Summit, if necessary, routine. Once at a meeting you asked her about folding underwear and socks, but only after you mentioned how happy you were with her independence in this area.

Now it's time to bring up the issue of Vigorous Independence Training (V.I.T.). Next, you ask her this question: "You're doing so well with your laundry, what would you like to do next on your own with absolutely no help from me?" Kylie is at a bit of a loss for how to answer the question, so you show her a copy of List A and List B. "Over here are things you'll want to learn to do for yourself as an adult (List A)," you explain, "and over here (List B) are things you might want to do for the rest of the family." Kylie looks at the list and picks Homework and Meal Prep.

Since you're still in your family meeting, you are free to ask a few questions regarding her choices. "How would it feel to you if I did not remind you about your homework? How would you remind yourself? Would you still want to show your work to me?" and so on. You do your best to let your daughter come up with the solutions, and you reinforce them. Kylie appears enthusiastic about the new way of doing things. You are also enthusiastic because you sense another one of your primary childcare jobs biting the dust. You both select next Monday as your starting date for her independent homework completion—the next step in your collaborative V.I.T. program.

On Monday and Tuesday Kylie appears to be doing well. She looks like she is in her room after school and part of the evening working on school stuff. You smile and say very little, other than "Looks like you're doing well." On Wednesday, though, your girl throws you a curve. She goes to a friend's house after school and for dinner, gets home late, then gets wrapped up in a TV special. You know she hasn't done a bit of homework, and you are nervous. Your old Mommy ID is prodding you to do your job, give your daughter a break, and remind her of what needs to be done.

Your new Mommy ID, though, says no. You're not trying to be cruel, but you're going to go with natural consequences. Learning from her own mistakes, not from parental lectures, is the best way for Kylie to learn. But you're nervous, and you don't know if you'll be able to sleep.

Kylie's bedtime is nine o'clock. At nine thirty she comes into your bedroom, panicked. "My homework isn't done!" she says. "Wow," you say. You give yourself an A+ for not doing any "I told you so" automatic talking.

"Can I stay up and do it?" she asks.

"I think it's better for you to get some sleep," you say, "even though you're a bit upset. You can get up earlier tomorrow and finish what you can."

The next morning Kylie gets up a half hour earlier. She finishes most, but not all, of her homework. "What am I going to tell my teacher?" she asks you.

"I'd just tell her the truth," you respond. "Tell her you and I are working on your doing homework on your own. You did very well the first two days, but last night you were busy and forgot. Everyone is entitled to a bad hair day now and then." Good response.

As Kylie heads off to school with some trepidation, you ask her to be sure to tell you how it goes with Ms. Mason. You know she will! As the door closes, your Mommy ID takes one last shot at you: "Kylie's teacher is going to think she doesn't have any mother!" You tell the creature inside to shut up.

Kylie is like a lot of kids. They thrive on independence, and they love being recognized for it when they get the chance. Let 'em run! What's next on Lists A and B? V.I.T is a lot of fun for everybody!

A Strange Conversation

One of the most interesting conversations I ever had occurred one afternoon at the American Academy of Pediatrics (AAP) trade show. Pediatricians love *1-2-3 Magic,* so we always have an exhibit booth each year in San Francisco, Boston, Orlando, or wherever they get together. At the show I get a chance to sign books for—and also talk to—hundreds of these hard-working, intelligent, and very altruistic physicians. They are always keenly interested in child discipline!

A few years ago I had a talk with a pleasant woman who stopped by for a book. She was a physician, but her job also involved overnight travel several days each week. She wanted to ask me a discipline question. It seems her family (husband and two kids, seven and ten) "drove her nuts" every morning during the process of their getting up and out to school. They just couldn't seem to get going.

"If it weren't for me getting after them all the time," she said, "I don't think they'd ever get anywhere!" she said. As we talked about this issue, she also mentioned that she travelled and was gone about two days per week on average. Most of these nights away were weeknights and school nights. I suddenly wondered to myself, "What do Dad and kids do about getting up and out when Mom is gone?" So I asked her as politely as I could.

"I don't know how they do it, but somehow they do," she said. "It's really amazing, when you think about it, because when I'm there they look almost incapable of doing anything!" The more we discussed this unique situation, the more it appeared like a Manager Mom problem. Dad and the children were actually different people when Mom was around—they were much more passive and waited for instructions before moving. Manager Mom, on the other hand, "accommodated" them by dishing out hurried and persistent directions in a flurry of automatic talking.

This was truly a Manager Mom and the Rest-of-the-Family Conspiracy. The more I talked to this doctor, the more it became apparent that her major motivations for her side of this unfortunate collaboration were kindness and anxiety! She was not a nasty person, and she sincerely wanted what was best for her family. That was to get the job (get everyone out in the morning) done and to get it done right (on time).

These mornings, of course, did nothing to enhance family bonding. Everyone was running on autopilot. Is Mom home this morning? If yes, it's Manager Mom time. Is Mom out of town? Then it's Dad's and kids' independence time.

Getting Out of Dodge (G.O.O.D.)

This AAP episode got me thinking. Is it possible that much of the time dads and kids actually have the autonomy and the skills necessary to carry off List A (self-care) and List B (household jobs) stuff even though they don't look like they do? Is it possible that they simply react automatically to Mom's presence by transforming themselves into passive, apathetic blobs who just wait for instructions? And is it possible that Manager Mom, seeing this passionless inactivity, responds by trying to assertively fill in the perceived responsibility gap?

The answer is yes. It happens a lot. That's the bad news. But this whole set up actually offers good news, because it points directly to a powerful Manager Mom firing strategy.

If you're a Manager Mom and you've just read this, you may be thinking "Well, I'm just going to tell everybody that from now on I'm no longer the President, Chief Servant, and First Responder! That'll do it!!" Maybe it will, maybe it won't. Your brief lecture, though, will probably be a bad start because it will just be perceived as more automatic talking. When they see you in the same room, they will very likely turn into passive blobs again.

There is a better way: Get Out of Dodge (G.O.O.D.). Remember the Kickoff, Let Go, Nonverbal Feedback, Summit sequence? Substitute Get Out of Dodge for the Kickoff. Leave town at the critical moment, leave everyone to their own devices, and see what happens!

I can feel Mommy IDs going crazy with bewilderment and irritation at this suggestion. What—you must be nuts! That's a total abdication of all motherly responsibility! Cruel and unusual punishment! Someone will get hurt! I wouldn't be able to look at myself in the mirror!

Well, let's examine this calmly. Example A: Let's imagine you have two toddlers ages two and four. Has a male of the species ever said to you on a Friday night "I'm part of a golf foursome tomorrow. We'll be doing eighteen holes. Will try to get back by one or two"? You have the kids for at least half the day, plus breakfast and lunch.

Now let's imagine you as part of that same family. On Friday night you announce to your spouse "Jill and I are going to the gym tomorrow at ten to work out. Then we're doing lunch at Michael's. Be back around 1:30." With these age kids, Dad will have a little primary childcare on his hands, won't he? Your goal here is not revenge. Your goal is to get a break and to foster dad-child bonding. G.O.O.D. is good for everybody!

Example B: You have a partner and kids ages twelve and sixteen. What would happen if you left the house early in the morning for work and let everyone else get up and out on their own, kind of like our AAP Mom? What if you did this as an experiment? What if you did a kind of Kickoff and told everyone what you were going to do and why? Then the evening after their independent up and out, you interviewed everyone separately (or together) in a kind of summit meeting, discussed how the morning went, then reinforced everyone's independence?

What comes next? Try G.O.O.D. again! Let dads and kids refine their morning procedures until you're completely out of the morning picture. Just keep leaving for work early until the rest of the gang masters the task themselves. Let them conquer the problem by means of a steady diet of natural consequences. All executive-functioning levels in this case are above age nine. Hmm.

The possibilities are numerous. What if you Got Out of Dodge

The technique of using your absence as a new learning-mastery experience for other family members has a lot of power.

at dinnertime on a weeknight and let everyone get his own food (cleanup to be discussed at a family meeting!)? What if you pumped enough breast milk for your two-month-old and left him in Dad's care while you and your seven-year-old did the trampoline place, dinner, and then ice cream?

Getting Out of Dodge will test your Mommy ID big time, and G.O.O.D. won't work for everything. It probably won't get a ten-year-old, for example, to clean her room. But the technique of using your absence as a new learning-mastery experience for other family members has a lot of power. And many of these options will help with accomplishing household tasks as well as with shedding the burden of unnecessary primary care. Getting Out of Dodge is not revenge, it's training. You may, though, get just a bit of perverse satisfaction out of it!

CHAPTER SUMMARY

Dads and kids often turn into passive blobs when Mom is present.

SEVENTEEN

Cooking, Food Shopping, and Housecleaning

IN THIS CHAPTER WE'LL LOOK at three tasks that Manager Mom is often overdoing and that dads and kids are often underdoing: cooking, shopping, and cleaning. We'll examine some ways of managing responsibility transfers in these areas. Then, since these three tasks involve the need for training kids and sometimes dads, we'll describe some friendly, painless, and many times fun ways of handling quality instructional efforts.

As always, our methods will focus not only on handing off jobs, but on doing so in ways that improve family bonding, achieve a more equitable distribution of labor, and help kids become more independent. Our biggest aces in the hole with these responsibilities are the facts that kids like one-on-one time with a parent, enjoy learning new skills, and like operating on their own. We don't want so much for Mom to get rid of cooking, shopping, and cleaning entirely. We do want dads and kids to pick up some of these responsibilities, and we want family members to enjoy these activities together at times.

Cooking

According to our available ATUS data, cooking—along with its inevitable counterpart, cleaning up the kitchen—can take up to a couple of hours per day. That's a lot of time. Lots of people, moms, kids, and dads, enjoy cooking a lot—it's creative, fun, and is a major contributor to the common good. What most people don't enjoy, however, is cooking all the time or cooking in a hurry right after coming home from work.

To get the mealtime ball rolling, let's imagine a mom who has been cooking pretty much every night for a family of four: Mom (Shae), Dad (Harley), nine-year-old Tabitha, and seven-year-old Cullen. Shae is tired of that much food preparation and cleanup. Shae and Harley both work full time, and Tabitha is now falling into our magic executive-functioning age of nine or older. Harley is in the ambivalent category, but he and his wife get along fairly well.

So Mom holds a family summit. She is aware that spontaneous, offhand comments about who's doing the cooking are too likely to be said in anger by her and not taken seriously by others. A planned get together is the way to go. At the family meeting Mom calmly and confidently declares that she is working full time and tired of cooking

seven nights a week. From now on, there will be the following schedule: Mom cooks two nights a week, Tabitha two nights, Dad two nights, and one night is every man for himself.

One thing that I have experienced with family meetings and training is this: Other family members will *always* have their own way of doing things. They will come up with ideas that are: 1) different from Mom's, 2) sometimes better than Mom's, and 3) they will often make what Mom may consider to be mistakes when carrying out a plan. It's very important, during meetings and trainings, to be open to all of these possibilities—and to be patient and flexible. Sometimes other people have a better way of doing things than you do, and sometimes they have methods that are just as good as yours, only different.

Dad's knee-jerk reaction to Mom's proposal, for example, is irritation. He didn't see this change coming. He comes back with a counter offer that for his nights he has the right to either bring back carry out or cook if he wants. Mom agrees. Tabitha is also a bit surprised, but she has enjoyed some of the cooking she

Sometimes other people have a better way of doing things than you do, and sometimes they have methods that are just as good as yours, only different.

has done in the past, so she's not irritated. Tabitha does have two questions, though. If Dad gets carry out, can they get what they want? And also, what about Cullen? Big sister senses a possible violation of the Equal Suffering Law here if her brother still gets fed every night but gets off free of any cooking responsibilities at the same time.

Dad agrees to consult family members before doing carry out. He says he may also cook sometimes. Mom tells Cullen that he is going into training. On some of her cooking nights, she and Cullen will cook together, and he can help decide what the meal will be.

Mom then adds, as an afterthought, that since Dad and Tabitha already have some of their own recipes, they can also help train Cullen to cook. Good idea, Mom thinks. Why do I have to be the First Responder again to the new problem of training my son in the kitchen? I don't.

The family summit has gone well. Mom is happy and relieved. The cooking schedule also opens up some food shopping possibilities that might be fun. But now this mom has another problem to confront: *herself.*

Shae's Mommy ID

To be able to present her proposal calmly and confidently at the family summit, Shae has to wrestle with herself a good deal—both before the meeting and after. As soon as she started thinking about cooking less and about asking other family members to cook more, her Maternal Identity started acting up. The attack consisted of the following thoughts:

1. It's my job to cook. I like feeding my own family! I'd feel like a slacker if I only cooked two suppers a week. My own mother cooked pretty much every night.

2. The kitchen can be dangerous. Two things in particular: knives and high temperatures. My husband might be OK, but I'm afraid my kids could get hurt. I'd feel terrible if they did! And what if they broke the oven?

3. The food won't be as good if I don't prepare it. No one in this family can or will ever cook as well as I do!

4. What will I tell my friends? They'll think I'm lazy. None of them cook only two times per week. You want to see a self-esteem problem? I'll soon have one!

Thoughts and feelings like these can be tough to deal with. Some women feel that if this is the cost of emancipation, the price is too high. And yet they also want more free time, and they would like their kids to learn to cook for themselves. In many homes, however, a strong maternal cooking identity results not so much in chronic supervision but rather in the exclusion from the kitchen of other family members.

It's also easy to imagine that maternal objections like Shae's could easily lead to automatic talking that could damage a family meeting or ruin attempts to train children to cook: "Watch what you're doing there!"; "Here, let me do that…"; "You put the pan in too soon—it's going to get all burned!";"It's just a whole lot easier if I do this myself!"

Shae, though, is really tired of being a Manager Mom. She's tired of resenting her own family. She's tired of an unbalanced division of household labor. And she wants her kids to learn to be independent and not drive their future partners or spouses crazy by being domestic weaklings.

Challenging the Mommy ID

Shae counters the objections of her Inner Mommy Cooking ID like this:

1. My mother cooked pretty much every night: Fine, but did my mother enjoy that? Would she have appreciated a break? Didn't I sometimes feel bad for her?

2. The kitchen can be dangerous: Of course it can, but I'm going to train my kids well. So well, as a matter of fact, that they'll soon be able to cook without me being in the kitchen at all while they're working.

3. The food won't be as good. That may be true for a while. But it will still most likely be OK-to-good, and it will serve its purpose—nourishment. Dad and the kids will get better at cooking, and they'll eventually provide more variety in what our family eats. Maybe one of the children will become a future chef!

4. My friends will think I'm lazy. I'll tell them the truth. They may be jealous! I'll be a good role model for them as a Manager Mom escapee! And my self-esteem should improve since I'll be doing the right thing for my kids—helping them to greater autonomy.

This successful challenge to Shae's Mommy ID allows her to not feel guilty and defensive when making her proposal to the rest of the family. That—plus the ESL being in the room with everyone—in turn allows especially Harley and Tabitha to talk and act reasonably.

Let's Go Food Shopping!

According to our available ATUS data, shopping—and especially food shopping—is a fairly sizeable, but not huge, user of a mom's time. On average, adults with children spend between 2–3 hours per week on "Consumer goods purchases," men coming in at right about two hours per week and women at right about three hours. So food shopping is not a super big job, but it's one that is inescapable and that has to be done regularly. Food shopping is also a task that lots of women and men enjoy a good deal of the time. Kids can also enjoy shopping a lot—especially when they're in charge of the trip!

Mom's food shopping time will probably decrease with the new home cooking schedule. But the new cooking arrangement also opens up some new possibilities that combine several of our other anti-Manager Mom tools: quality training, the

Kids can enjoy shopping a lot—especially when they're in charge of the trip!

Divide and Conquer Routine (family bonding), use of Dad's secondary childcare time, and well-designed training.

Tools: Quality Training

Here's how it works. Mom and Tabitha—or rather, Tabitha with consultation from Mom—picks two four-course meals that she would like to cook for the family. While her daughter brainstorms the meals, Mom tries to remain as quiet and passive as she can. She only talks or offers advice if and when Tabitha gets stuck. This girl does not get stuck. She likes designing a meal by herself. Her first four-course selection consists of these items:

- Boneless, skinless chicken thighs
- Chicken-flavored rice
- Frozen peas
- Applesauce

The second consists of these items:

- Salmon with brown-sugar glaze
- Sliced tomatoes
- Boiled new potatoes
- Fresh broccoli

Now Mom and her daughter will go shopping for all this stuff. This is an opportunity to use the Divide and Conquer Routine. It's an extra bonus—it will be Girls' Night Out. Just the two of them!

The outing will also represent good training for Tabitha as far as shopping is concerned. Mom and daughter can further discuss cooking meals while they are shopping. Since Tabitha has adequate executive-functioning abilities, Tabitha does the menu, Tabitha makes the shopping list, Tabitha leads the way in the grocery store and finds everything herself.

Mom follows Tabitha and keeps quiet unless absolutely necessary. When Tabitha makes a wrong turn on the way from chicken to rice, for example, Mom will say nothing and follow obediently and quietly. Her daughter can read the signs and noodle it out. Mom gives daughter either a credit card or cash so Tabitha—not Mom—can pay the bill. Mom, of course, may have to sign.

You'll notice this whole setup is the opposite of the Manager Mom Syndrome. Tabitha is the leader, Mom the follower. This is good training for both of them, even though it is not particularly efficient in the beginning. Too often, you will recall, the Manager Mom Syndrome dictates that it is Mom's supervisory responsibility to see that the job gets done *now* and gets done *right*—Mom's way—regardless of the feelings of other family members. That is what automatic talking is all about.

If Mom talks too much during menu creation or list making, or she starts barking when her daughter makes a wrong turn in Aisle 9, you will be able to observe Tabitha's enthusiasm wilting in direct proportion to the volume of her mother's oratory. During responsibility transfers, a little inefficiency is critical in the beginning in order to maintain kids' interest, energy, and ownership. (A couple of cute and helpful books along these lines are *The Complete Cookbook for Young Chefs* and *The Stepstool Chef Cookbook for Kids*).

The Icing on the Cake: Shared One-on-One Fun

But the daughter and mom in our scenario are not done yet! For this outing, Mom and Tabitha design their shopping trip to include dinner. And, to make matters more interesting, they go to their favorite barbecue place *before* shopping and on a *weekday*. That means they're gone at dinnertime. They're going to tap into Dad's secondary childcare skills and availability. He has to be home anyway, and now he only has to care for one child, Cullen.

Dad and his son are on their own!? Great—the boys can fend for themselves, and at home we'll hopefully see another nice example of pair bonding—and, in this instance, also a case of that very necessary and often ignored dad-child bonding. Maybe there's a good game on. Maybe they can go to the gym. It will be a wonderful evening for all: Mom, Dad, daughter, and son. I guarantee it!

Next time Dad and Mom may switch kids: Dad is with Tabitha, Mom is with Cullen. Recall that Cullen is in cooking training which, of course, will involve shopping too.

It's also true that lots and lots of dads enjoy cooking and shopping. At our house I do most of the cooking and cleanup, using about ten basic recipes. With that number, no one meal gets repeated too often. So for Shae's family, Harley could share with Tabitha some of his recipes—and the two of them could go out shopping for those meals. Harley—or Shae—could also do the same with Cullen. Ease off the whole-family fun compulsion and all kinds of good things can happen. Pair bonding rules!

Housecleaning

Housecleaning seems to be a task that no one wants to do. Who wants to vacuum or dust, for example, and who wants to clean a bathroom or a toilet? It may surprise you to learn that there are lots of adults—and some kids—who actually find cleaning house satisfying. They enjoy the place looking nice after their efforts are completed. In fact, if you are interested, there's a very entertaining book called *Is There Life After Housework: A Revolutionary Approach to Cutting Your Cleaning Time by 75%* by Don Aslett which states just that: people can enjoy cleaning! The author also points out that cleaning can be done in much more efficient ways that—according to this author—can reduce cleaning time significantly.[26]

In order to deal with housecleaning, I think the job needs to be divided up into three categories, which often require different tactics. These categories are keeping one's own bedroom picked up, keeping the public areas in the house picked up, and real cleaning (vacuuming, dusting, toilets, bathrooms, etc.). All three tasks are good candidates for family or one-on-one meetings, which can also be done by text or phone.

Kids' bedrooms. If a child is already keeping a pretty neat room, start by reinforcing that fact by praising them in a way they find acceptable. Don't give syrupy praise, for example, to a teen or to a businesslike kid. If their room is typically a mess, use the Close the Door and Don't Look routine from *1-2-3 Magic* while you work on the other two categories, picking up the house and cleaning.

If you simply can't stand their mess, consider using a Weekly Cleanup routine, but only as a last resort. You and your child agree that their weekend activities (including computer, friends, and TV) don't start on Saturday until after their room is cleaned according to your specifications. Make the rules clear and don't argue about them at checkout time. Praise good performance.

Picking up the house. Ideally, you'll want a daily routine for keeping the house picked up. Otherwise the place soon looks like it's out of control. Keep in mind, though, that if keeping the joint picked up is not really a big part of your Mommy ID, there's no law in your state saying you have to do it or get others to cooperate. If you'd like things picked up more regularly, at a family meeting propose the Kitchen Timer and Docking System or the Garbage Bag Method.

With the Docking System if you have to pick up their stuff after a certain time each evening, they pay you for that effort. In addition, you can put their things into a 55-gallon drum in the garage or temporarily in a big plastic bag. Things in the bag are unavailable to them for one or two days (except school material). Once again, just do it—no arguing or lectures filled with righteous indignation.

"Real" housecleaning. A family summit is a good place to divide up and rotate chores among Mom, Dad, and kids. You can change each week or each month who does the vacuuming, dusting, garbage removal, bathrooms, toilets, and so on. Try to take into account at your family conferences who likes to do what. I knew a guy once who actually enjoyed cleaning toilets! You can also discuss whether or not you want to consider a cleaning person coming in on a regular basis.

> **Many moms feel forced to change their standards for what a "clean enough" house is.**

In the big, bad, and real world, many moms feel forced to change their standards for what a "clean enough" house is. Although it may sound funny, *lowering* your housecleaning standards is a perfectly legitimate option. Instead of feeling badly about yourself, your house, and your family every day, accept the new reality even though it may not match the way you grew up. You can set the bar wherever you want to—we're not talking about federal law. Challenge that aspect of your Mommy ID, reset, and relax!

Good Training Means...

Whether it's cooking, food shopping, or dusting, responsibility transfers to other family members often involve training them to do what

Mom has been doing. Here's a summary of some of the factors that make for good training that really takes hold:

1. See what skills and knowledge other family members already have, and reinforce those strengths with praise. Then fill in the gaps where necessary.
2. Let kids or dads run the show as much as possible.
3. Go slowly. Show how the job is to be done then let the other person try.
4. Remain silent as much as you can.
5. Look for times where a dad or child is doing something differently from you but in a way that's just as effective as what you do. Reinforce their creativity.
6. Be gentle about mistakes. Training is necessary because people are not as skilled as you are at doing certain things.
7. Allow for considerable sloppiness and inefficiency in preschoolers, and try to reinforce their enthusiasm.
8. Never train when you're rushed, tired, or crabby.
9. Whenever possible, treat trainings as one-on-one fun times— even with dads!

CHAPTER SUMMARY

The fact that lots of adults and children like food shopping and cooking— plus the added fun of one-on-one bonding—can add tons of motivational power to getting these jobs done. Housecleaning is admittedly a tougher nut to crack, but that task can also benefit from those same basic incentives. Imagine shopping and cooking morphing from chores to pastimes!

Tabitha's Four-Course Dinner

- Boneless, skinless chicken thighs
- Chicken-flavored rice
- Frozen peas
- Applesauce

YUM!

PART IV

TODDLERS TO TEENS

Designing Away the Manager Mom Syndrome

EIGHTEEN

Preschoolers: Craziness, Precedents, and Sloppy Training

ONE OF THE HARDEST THINGS anyone will ever do in his or her life is bring their first child home from the hospital. The experience is very different from what our culture leads us to believe it will be like. Just the other day, one veteran mom said to me, "Why didn't they tell me what it was going to be like with a brand-new baby!? I was totally unprepared. Yeah, there was some excitement and even a sense of awe, but there was also extreme mental fatigue, physical fatigue, irritation and drudgery."

After going through a physical event that amounts to major surgery, Mom is exhausted and the new baby's feeding schedule often keeps her in a state of sleep deprivation for many weeks. Mom's primary support staff, Dad, is also in a state of shock. Though he is proud of his new son or daughter, he suddenly feels left out due to the close connection between Mom and baby. While Mom has been bonding with the child for nine months, Dad has not. A new father often sees the new child as a kind of stranger as well as an intruder into the family. Dad suddenly has mixed feelings toward his wife, and he feels like a third wheel in his own house.

After a few weeks of this new regime, Mom and Dad will have completed their transition from lovers to parents. They are not as close as they were, they pay less positive attention to each other, and it seems their lives are now dominated by the new little creature at home. Unfortunately, it's a great time for the Manager Mom Syndrome to take root.

New Baby, Hard Work!

The days and weeks after baby comes home are a time of critical precedent setting as far as Manager Mom is concerned. Who is going to do what—Mom or Dad? Newborns don't do much other than eat, sleep, cry, and poop, but in the beginning these primary childcare responsibilities usually fall entirely on the mother. After caring for the baby in her stomach for nine months, Mom will likely continue to be the First Responder in the household to the baby's needs.

The days and weeks after baby comes home are a time of critical precedent setting as far as Manager Mom is concerned.

Three-quarters of moms in this country choose to breastfeed, and dad can't provide that service. When the baby cries or wakes, Mom will go see what is the matter. When a diaper needs changing, Mom will usually change it. There is a natural—and in some ways logical—progression from carrying the baby around inside to caring for the baby once it is outside. This burden for Mom often includes the new household tasks associated with a new baby, such as extra laundry, bottle washing, and shopping.

So there is a strong tendency—unless a serious family meeting intervenes or paternity leave is available to fathers after a baby is born—for moms to First Respond to primary childcare tasks (feeding, diaper-changing, sleep issues), secondary childcare (remaining in the house with the baby), and household baby-related chores. Mom will take on these jobs because that's the powerful precedent (childcare is Mom's job) that existed in the house (and inside Mom!) for the last nine months. This precedent—and how it might be modified—are issues that are rarely discussed between moms and dads.

Can Dad actually help with feedings and diapers? Yes, but often other factors block a more fair distribution of labor. Many experts, for example, feel that dads can bottle-feed a baby with Mom's breast milk after about a month. This transition requires the patient, sensitive, and careful training of three people. First, the baby has to adjust to a bottle and to being held and fed by a different adult. It's often best for Mom to introduce Baby to bottle first, so the child only has to get used to Dad (with bottle) afterwards. Second, Dad has to get trained. He must learn to prepare a bottle and how to hold and feed the baby. After a while, many dads can enjoy this experience and it makes for good dad-child bonding.

Last, but definitely not least, Mom also has to be trained to adjust to the new dad-child feeding arrangement. She must adjust to giving up some of her feeding function (check with Mommy ID), at least some of the time. You recall that Manager Mom's thinking focuses on getting a job done now and getting it done right. As we have seen, this maternal orientation can seriously interfere with successful responsibility transfers. If Dad fumbles a bit with the bottle, or the milk's not warm enough, or baby cries a bit with Dad, it's not hard for some moms to think *It's just a lot easier if I do it myself!* What happens then? A responsibility does not get transferred, and the burden stays with Mom.

The same kind of thinking can occur with diapers. Many moms think *Dad won't change the diaper as well as I will. He'll leave a dirty one on too long, or he may not put it on right, thus allowing for blowouts through the sides. It's easier if I do it.* Another point for Manager Mom.

Fortunately, if the situation is handled patiently and intelligently, babies are usually pretty flexible in adapting to different folks doing feedings and changings. To prevent the initiation of Manager Mom during the first few months of baby's being home, Mom and Dad need to be cooperative and adaptable. If Mom's Mommy ID is too rigid, for example, instead of gently training Dad, she will not allow him to take over some of these basic primary childcare jobs. Do it *now* and do it *right* is the motto!

How will Dad react to this? The restriction of his new learning and the retraction of a new potential skill will make Dad feel insulted. Unfortunately, however, he will also be relieved. Unlike his First Responder spouse, he may not react aggressively to baby problems and he'll be happy to remain in the background if he is allowed—or compelled—to. Dad will not realize at this early stage that he will later be resented for this ESL violation (unequal primary childcare time). In addition, Mom and Dad will inadvertently have conspired to create the Manager Mom Syndrome and a great opportunity for father-child bonding will have been missed.

So new baby equals a tough time and a lot of hard work. The vast majority of parents, however, say that they would have kids again—even knowing how hard of a job it was. Why? It's a high-cost, but also a high-reward activity. The other side of the trauma is that first smile at two months, the giggle, the love of fun, kids' curiosity, the fact of that really cute little face, and children's natural "ability" to take us adults back to the wonder of our own childhoods. And a lot more.

The First-Month Precedents

In order to avoid the development of Manager Mom, therefore, in the first month after the arrival of the new baby we want to avoid the powerful precedents that seem to naturally deposit primary childcare, secondary childcare, and baby-related household tasks into Mom's lap. These precedents are Mom's having carried the baby for nine months, Mom's likely being the chief feeder, and Mom's natural First Responder tendencies. If a couple is not careful, these patterns can predispose Mom and Dad to a very lopsided distribution of child-care (and household) responsibilities that persists for as long as the children are living at home.

Some fortunate couples, without discussing the issues out loud too much, seem to spontaneously evolve into a fairly equal distribution of all the new tasks. In these cases, Dad is usually not a super-traditionalist dad, and Mom's Mommy ID is open to responsibility transfers that are not perfect. Gentle, patient training of Mom, Dad, and baby takes place.

In other situations, chance may intervene. One mom I spoke with had had a C-section, so she could not change the diapers of her new eight-pound daughter. Dad took over, and Mom had to admit, after a while, "He's a better diaper-changer than I am."

In other families, events don't proceed so smoothly. As one mother said, "I have always gotten up at night with the kids. It started when the first one came home from the hospital and I was breastfeeding. I was the go-to night person. I was exhausted those first months. I felt like the baby monitor dominated my life, but not my husband's."

Another important factor that can affect the development of the Manager Mom Syndrome is cultural. There are quite a few countries where parenting satisfaction is much higher than it is in the United States. Many of these places are in Scandinavia. What do these countries have there that we don't have here? They have liberal maternity leave (often one year), fairly liberal paternity leave (several months), and subsidized child daycare.

What do these benefits do? It's very simple. They give parents—especially moms—a break from the kids. Though children are lovable, entertaining, and outrageously cute, they are permanent, demanding, and unrelenting. Although babies sleep a ton, they require constant secondary childcare, lots of primary care, and they double the household workload.

A social system like Sweden's, for example, allows for simultaneous maternity and paternity leave, so primary and secondary childcare jobs—theoretically at least—can be split up between Mom and Dad as soon as the baby comes home. Mom's mental health requires her being able to get away from the kids for several hours at a time. Sweden's system allows for the possibility of setting this kind of "mom can split" precedent during the first month of baby's being home.

Mom can Get Out of Dodge and leave baby and spouse. Dad does feedings, diapers, and is present for emergencies during the day. Equally important, though, is the possibility that baby's nighttime needs can also be divided between parents since neither of them is required to go to work for the first few months. This helps prevent the all-too-common problem of maternal sleep deprivation.

Toddlers: Let the Madness Begin!

While infants are a lot of work, seriously impair their parents' freedom, and contribute to sleep deprivation, they at least cooperate to some extent by staying put and sleeping a lot. They aren't able to climb out of their cribs or playpens. You usually find them where you last left them.

As children get older, though, they start crawling, then staggering, then walking, then running. They don't sleep so much (60 percent of children stop naps by age three), and they no longer cooperate so well with their parents' concerns about their safety—or their parents' concerns with anything, for that matter. Kids are active, curious explorers, and during that second year they really, really start wanting to do things their own way.

Toddlers and preschoolers also have about zip in the way of executive-functioning abilities. They can't keep much of a plan in their heads or carry out the sequence of activities necessary to complete the plan. That's why we get so many emails from frustrated parents asking "Why can't my three-year-old clean up his own room?" He can't clean up his room because he is three.

For parents, the new life these developmental stages usher in is another era of mixed blessings. As one mom put it, "It's nuts!" Extreme cuteness, great fun, and lots of affection mixed with new behaviors like tantrums, whining, hyperactivity, and not wanting to stay in bed. To put it simply: These kids are a ton of fun, but you don't necessarily want to spend your whole day being with them. Lots of parents feel bad admitting this. They feel they are saying they don't love their children. It's nothing of the kind. Recall Patterson's *Mothers: The Unacknowledged Victims*: kids can be hard to be with! Also recall parents' ratings of their favorite activities. Preschoolers are both very entertaining and very stressful, so too many parents overdose on that package!

In Sweden, parents have access to subsidized childcare. They don't have to spend all day every day with their small children. Not only that, these parents can get their old jobs back! Their employer has to hold their position for them while they are out on leave, and the person who replaced them has to either take another job or leave the company. Incredible—whose idea was this? Nothing like this is available in the U.S. on any kind of widespread basis.

That's why parenting satisfaction in Sweden is so much higher than it is here. Parents, especially moms, don't overdose on their kids, and the danger of Manager Mom Syndrome is much less because of the simultaneous maternity and paternity leaves.

Prevention and Precedent

To prevent the Manager Mom Syndrome from developing during the kids' 0–5 years, and to prevent general insanity, the following recommendations are super important:

1. Dangerous ESL precedents can be set during the first month after baby comes home. Family summits regarding the imminent domestic labor explosion should occur before baby is born!

2. Mommy ID issues can be even touchier right after the birth of a baby—especially the first baby. Make sure you get your Maternal Identity straightened around before any summit meetings with dads. Your motto should be confident and decisive rather than guilty and anxious! The Equal Suffering Law is real and it is reasonable.

3. Gently train Dad during the first month in bottle-feeding,

204 | The Best Moms Don't Do It All

> *Parents—especially moms—need extended breaks from their children under age six.*

diaper-changing, and nighttime intervention tactics. Maternal sleep deprivation needs to be avoided as much as possible.

4. Parents—especially moms—need extended breaks from their children under age six, during the day and also at night. After quality diaper and bottle training, exploit Dad's secondary childcare availability—and primary care skills!

5. The Divide and Conquer Routine is very valuable for families with preschoolers. Dyadic events reduce family stress and allow for more dad-child, mom-child, and dad-mom bonding. Make sure whole-family activities are mixed with liberal doses of pair-bonding times.

CHAPTER SUMMARY

During the preschool years moms need to use G.O.O.D. (Get Out of Dodge) to find alone time for themselves as well as one-on-one time with individual children. Trust the male of the species to take adequate care of the children.

NINETEEN

Ages Six through Nine: Basic Training

THE PRESCHOOL YEARS ARE THE often-enjoyable-but-also-crazy years. These years involve a lot of hard work and stress for a young couple, with most of it often falling on Mom's shoulders. Dads and moms during this time also set critical precedents for who is going to be handling what when it comes to primary childcare, secondary childcare, and household responsibilities.

With their limited executive functioning skills, preschoolers can't—on their own—start and finish tasks such as getting dressed, getting to bed, picking up their toys, and sometimes eating meals. And if they can't do these things, they certainly can't do jobs like laundry, cooking, and cleaning (though they can try!).

Nine-year-olds, however, *can* handle these more advanced tasks. It's just that we don't expect them to, and we don't really let them. We unwittingly, therefore, let a major solution to the Manager Mom problem slip through our fingers without even realizing what we're doing. We put more pressure on the mom vs. dad labor-sharing problem. We also damage family affection and put an artificial ceiling on children's independence.

A New Goal Is Essential

So our question becomes this: How do you help your children progress over the years from total dependence to independence? The first step in the process is to set kids' independence as the goal for you and your children. That is a challenge for many American parents. Manager Moms, with dads' approval, set for themselves a goal of children's cooperation with parental direction. That's very different from seeing your ultimate objective as being children's self-direction.

In our country, we do not think it is unusual or odd that a parent would both prompt and supervise the homework of a fifteen-year-old. We don't think it's strange that a parent would wake up an eighteen-year-old on a school day. We tell our teens what to wear to school, we tell them to finish their supper, and we instruct them when to brush their teeth. Then we expect them to cooperate—cheerfully—even though they've just been insulted.

Kids cooperating with parental directives means chronic supervision. That's what the dean from Wakeful State was pointing out to the parents of his first-year students that we saw at the beginning of the book. That kind of cooperation, although nice, should be seen as a temporary phase *on the way to* total independence. Otherwise, you are simply perpetuating Manager Mom by perpet-

> *Our new goal has to be teaching our kids how to be self-starters rather than simply cooperative responders.*

uating unnecessary primary childcare. And if you treat primary childcare issues like that, you are certainly not going to get very far in getting kids to take over—not just help with—household responsibilities. Why? Because you are constantly reminding the children that you think they are incompetent and in need of your direction.

So our new goal has to be teaching our kids how to be self-starters rather than simply cooperative responders.

Interim Strategies for Ages 5–9

The typically developing nine-year-old has the cognitive skills to handle all the tasks and activities on our List A:

Getting dressed	Personal hygiene
Getting up and out in the morning	Finishing homework
Going to bed	Staying in bed after bedtime
Caring for pets	Picking up your stuff
Cleaning your bedroom	Eating

A typical nine-year-old can also manage these List B jobs:

Laundry	Housecleaning
Food prep and cleanup	Shopping

After the chaotic preschool years, from ages about five through nine, how do we get the kids to do both List A and List B jobs without parental prompting and supervision? We are going to do two things:

1. *Parents In:* As we discussed in Chapter 14, we are going to employ creative brainstorming and friendly experimentation to first get the kids to cooperate *with parental assistance.* We will escape anger paralysis, for example, by using *1-2-3 Magic*, other parenting programs, or even Google to generate new possible solutions to issues like homework, bedtime, or eating.

2. *Parents Out:* Then, as the children get closer to age nine, we are going to deliberately and systematically *phase Mom and Dad out of the picture,* so the kids are doing everything—prompting, progress monitoring, and finishing—on their own.

How will you know how successful you're being in your training efforts? You'll know by means of two very simple criteria. First, are the kids getting the jobs done? Second, are the jobs getting done with minimal or no automatic talking? Roughly speaking, parental monitoring, including prompts, guidance, and reinforcement, is still useful before the children reach age nine. After that, with the tweens and teens, we want parental intervention nonexistent and kids' independence maximized.

Then, as the children get closer to age nine, we are going to deliberately and systematically phase Mom and Dad out of the picture.

People often ask, "What about special needs children, such as those with attention deficit hyperactivity disorder (ADHD) or those with cognitive impairments? Do these broad age groupings still apply?" The answer in many cases is no, they do not apply. This will be true where the child's disability directly impacts their executive functioning skills. ADHD, for example, is often described as exactly that: an executive-skills deficit. These children have problems with working memory, sequencing tasks, and following through without distraction.

For children with ADHD, therefore, and other kids with special needs, we often use what we call the 30 Percent Rule.[27] Say you have a child with ADHD who is twelve. Subtract 30 percent off from twelve and you get 8.4. What is 8.4? A more accurate age estimate of the emotional maturity, behavioral maturity, and executive-functioning skills of that child. When would we expect that boy with ADHD to achieve some substantial List A and List B independence? Around age fifteen or sixteen.

Basic Training for 6–9 Year Olds

So you are going to train your children ages six to nine to handle their self-care, List A stuff. You will need to do some prompting and monitoring for a while, but you will avoid useless automatic talking and silly defaults to reasoning. How? Well, you are going to set up and agree upon *routines* that your children will follow to carry out these tasks, which I discuss in much more detail in *1-2-3 Magic*. To help set up these routines you will use a number of very helpful and friendly tactics:

Praise or positive reinforcement   Docking System
Simple requests   Natural Consequences
Timers   Charting

Once you define a routine, it's a good idea to rehearse it with the kids. With a bedtime routine, for example, you might actually have the kids go through the ritual of brushing teeth, putting on pajamas, and checking in with you for a story before bed. But it's three o'clock in the afternoon on a Saturday! "Isn't this silly! We've got our pj's on during the daytime!" It's fun, but it helps the kids learn the procedure, which will reduce the pressure you feel to do automatic talking!

Then you're going to define and rehearse routines for staying in bed, homework, eating, and other positive behavior. Remember that rehearsal and routine greatly reduces the need you will feel to chatter when crunch time comes. Automatic talking reduces kids' willingness to cooperate by irritating them and makes everyone's job a lot harder by killing off affection and independence. Well-rehearsed routines help foster kids' autonomy.

CHAPTER SUMMARY

Shoot for age nine for basic independence!

TWENTY

Touchy Teens?
Time for Independence

W HILE THEY ARE GROWING UP, you'll find there are two times during children's lives when they are ferocious about asserting their desire for independence: the first period is the toddler-preschooler years, and the second period is the adolescent years. And when it comes to their own autonomy, toddlers are noisy-ferocious and teens are quiet-ferocious.

As we saw Chapter 18, toddlers will produce horrible tantrums when you don't let them do what they want, which is often "what the big people are doing." That's why you want to tap into their desire to help at an early age. Even though it may be a bit messy, let them put the dressing on the salad, put their dishes in the dishwasher, and help clean the toilets.

Teens—most of them, anyway—don't throw fierce temper tantrums like preschoolers do. But underneath their complacent and often somber exteriors, teens too are ferocious about their independence and about doing what adults are doing. They would like to manage their own money, drive their own car, pick their own friends, and contribute to their world.

How do we adults respond to teens' desires for independence and their altruistic strivings? Not very well, I'm afraid. In fact, teens become a big part of the Manager Mom problem, and no one—adolescent or parent—seems to know quite what to do about it.

Evening Stalemate

Imagine an evening dinner table scene. Two parents are sitting at the table with their sixteen-year-old son. Like most parents, these two adults want to strike up a pleasant conversation and also, maybe, just check to make sure their "child" is doing OK.

The conversation goes like this:

Mom to son: How was your day?

Son: Fine.

Mom: What'd you do?

Son: Nothin'.

Well, not a very good start. So Dad decides to help out a bit:

Dad to son: You have social studies?

Son: Yeah.

Dad: What'd you do in social studies?

Son: We didn't do nothin' in social studies.

Strike three for Mom and Dad. What's the problem? There are two problems here. The first is that this boy is ferociously asserting his independence. He doesn't want his parents' snooping condescension, and he doesn't want them messing around with his life. He translates their question "How was your day?" into this question: "Did you screw up anything today that we need to know about?"

And he refuses to answer. His behavior borders on rude and he is, in fact, irritated. He's thinking, "You don't need to butt into my affairs. I can handle everything myself." Read: *I can handle everything you bigger people can handle. Leave me alone.*

That's normal adolescence. Conversations like this one may go on each night in over twenty million American households. These conversations are common in industrialized countries where children—instead of working right away—have to spend many years in school in order to learn the various skills required for entering their societies' respective job markets. They consequently go through a long period of time where they are dependent upon their parents for food, shelter, and clothing.

To the Extent They Are Able

This leads to the second problem. We saw before that the average nine-year-old has the executive-functioning ability to do all kinds of things that we don't let them do. In addition, adding to the perception of adolescents' capabilities is the fact that these "kids" are now physically just as big—or almost as big—as their parents are. Everyone knows what these young people could, but aren't allowed, to do.

It's obvious to everybody, therefore, that these teenagers—these big, capable people—are evolutionary cheaters. Remember the phrase *contribute to the common good to the extent that they are able*? Adolescents are not doing that. Instead, Mom and Dad make the money. They buy the house or pay the rent, pay for leisure, food, clothes, and schoolbooks. In addition, they (though, of course, more often Mom) cook the food, wake the kids up for school, do the laundry, supervise homework, and drive the kids to soccer.

The "How was your day?" comment was addressed to a teen who knows he's a cheater, and he's mad about it. He's also embarrassed. His parents know he's a cheater, and they're trying to be nice about it. But nobody's fixing the problem! As a matter of fact, a common Manager Mom "solution" for dealing with an uncommunicative, sullen adolescent is often for Mom to try to do more for—and be nicer to—her teen.

Trivial Solutions for Frustrated Idealism

When we adults run across teenagers who don't talk, who look funny, and who seem to adore horrible music, we are often guilty of totally misinterpreting their behavior. We see teens as self-absorbed and as selfish. There may be some truth to those opinions. But the fact of the matter is that adolescents are also among the most idealistic

There's a big difference between what constitutes a meaningful contribution in the eyes of different people or family members.

people in the world. They have strong opinions about how the world should be run, and they are very altruistic—they want very much to do something to contribute, to help other people, and to make the world a better place. Like any adult, they want to feel needed by their family and by the community that they are a part of.

But there's a big difference between what constitutes a meaningful contribution in the eyes of different people or family members. An adolescent might see his or her Manager Mom running around frantically doing all kinds of household chores, as well as working outside the home full time. What does Manager Mom ask of him in return? Clean your room and take out the garbage. Then, when it seems that even these tasks are beyond the adolescent's capabilities, Mom concludes that the child is of no help, and she still has to "do everything around here." In reality, the adolescent sees these garbage and room cleaning as trivial and as not constituting a meaningful contribution.

Real Contributions

What *would* feel more meaningful for everyone? You've perhaps heard suggestions for how teens can feel more involved or contribute more. These include volunteer at a soup kitchen, become a lifeguard, tutor young children, or join a human rights coalition. All these are fine ideas and all have been done.

But our problem here is this: What would help an adolescent to go from a cheater role to a contributor role at home—*within his or her own family group*? Cleaning one's room or taking out the garbage are OK, but they don't quite cut it. Let's rephrase the question again: How can a teen help significantly reduce the Manager Mom burden for his own mother in ways that she would really appreciate?

Fortunately, the framework we've been discussing here offers three concrete answers that *all involve responsibility transfers*: 1) eliminate unnecessary primary childcare related to a particular teenager, 2) take over (not just "help with") basic household responsibilities, and 3) do some secondary childcare if there are younger siblings at home.

Eliminate Primary Childcare. On paper, this solution is pretty easy to describe and identify. It will be harder in practice, and Manager Mom will probably have to initiate the retraining process. Is Mom involved in waking up a teen for school? That's primary care for a "child" who doesn't need it, and it's an extra mental burden for Mom. How to do the handoff? Use the procedure that Willa's parents used in Chapter 13. Follow it to the letter to ensure a successful *total transfer* of the accountability for getting up and out in the morning!

Here's another example: Is Manager Mom supervising a teen's homework? Unless you have a special needs child, this shouldn't be necessary for an adolescent. Use the Natural Consequences procedure that Max's parents were considering. Let homework completion be a task supervised by child and teacher, not parents. Intervene only if something horrible is occurring.

How about other areas such as personal hygiene, dress, breakfast? Those should be left up to the teen and not Manager Mom. Parents will still have house rules for hours, cell phone use, use of the car, and bedtime. You can use family summits till those are all ironed out, then back off and get out of the primary childcare area. How does a mom know when she's successfully done that? By the quantity of automatic talking she's offering unnecessarily to her large-bodied, capable offspring.

Household Tasks. Taking out the garbage is fine, and it is a contribution to the common welfare. But it only takes three minutes to accomplish and generally happens only once a week. More meaningful contributions include adolescents doing their own laundry. Also, as we've seen in our case examples, a teen can give Manager Mom a break by cooking for the entire family (or getting carryout) on specified days of the week. Teens also easily meet the executive functioning requirements for being able to do food shopping, and they very likely will enjoy that task. Imagine a teenager making a food shopping list, buying the things on the list, cooking that meal for the whole family, then cleaning the kitchen afterwards. Now there's an anti–Manager Mom Syndrome contribution that is meaningful!

Finally, how about a kid who cleans the bathroom once a week, including scrubbing out the toilet! That's an expression of altruism.

Secondary Childcare. Teens are also old enough to do some babysitting of their own siblings. This is similar to the ATUS secondary childcare category that involves only parents. The idea is, basically, to have someone in the house who can handle emergencies. Sibling rivalry can remain a problem, of course, but in my experience kids usually get along better when their parents aren't around. But having a teen at home, like having a dad at home, can open up free-time opportunities for Manager Mom such as working out, just going for a walk or a drive, or getting together with friends.

Before you use a teen in a secondary childcare role, check out the vigilance section of your Mommy ID beforehand. If you recall, the Ninth Commandment went like this:

Vigilance. The world is a dangerous place, and I need to be hyper-vigilant for signs of danger to my kids. I should constantly worry and scan the physical and psychological environment for signs of trouble.

Can a typical fifteen-year-old babysit her twelve-year-old brother and eight-year-old sister for three hours? The answer is probably yes. Take a deep breath, relax, then go enjoy yourself!

P.S. Here's one final meaningful contribution some teens can make, and, surprisingly, it involves *primary* childcare. Adolescents with their drivers' licenses can drive younger sibs all over creation and back. And they will volunteer to do it! It's a real blessing for Manager Mom.

Sixteen-Year-Old Collin's Self-Esteem at 6:30 p.m.

Now let's revisit our "How was your day?" scene from the beginning of the chapter. Let's name the sixteen-year-old Collin. Collin is in the cheater category. He knows it, and his parents know it. They do everything for him around the house, and they pay for everything:

Mom: Collin, how was your day?

Collin: Fine.

Mom: What did you do?

Collin: Nothin'.

Dad: You have social studies?

Collin: Yeah.

Dad: Well, what did you do in social studies?

Collin: We didn't do nothin' in social studies.

What kind of spirits is Collin in during this interchange? How's his self-esteem? The answers are obvious from his behavior. Bad and bad.

Now imagine the scene below after the Manager Mom Syndrome has been seriously attacked and modified in this household. Collin is now contributing meaningfully by cooking twice a week, on Tuesdays and Fridays. Here's a new scene:

Vicky: Where's Mom?

Collin: She went out to dinner and a movie with a friend.

Vicky: Is it your night to cook?

Collin: Yep.

Reese (runs into kitchen): Collin, can you make your tacos?

Collin: Yeah, I can.

Vicky, Reese: Awright!!

Dad: Hey—don't forget about your old man. Make sure you make enough for me, too. I could eat a horse!

What kind of spirits is Collin in during this interchange? How's his self-esteem? The answers are good and good. What a difference between "Fine, nothin', fine, nothin'" vs. "Yeah, I can"!

If you have teens, the answer to Manager Mom and the solution to a lot of adolescent issues are intertwined in the question of what makes for a meaningful contribution from a teen to the family group he's a part of. To paraphrase John F. Kennedy's famous declaration during his 1961 inaugural address: Ask not what Manager Mom can do for you, ask what you can do for Manager Mom. Let's work toward little or no unnecessary primary childcare with our teens.

Ask not what Manager Mom can do for you, ask what you can do for Manager Mom.

CHAPTER SUMMARY

Teens are among the most idealistic people on the planet. And they cherish meaningful, competent independence.

TWENTY-ONE

After Manager Mom

OVER THE YEARS YOU'RE GOING to prevent the onset of the Manager Mom Syndrome with your younger kids and fire Manager Mom with your older children.

Making the transition from Manager Mom to non-Manager Mom will be an interesting one for you. The change will be full of surprises, it will involve lots of mixed feelings, and it will be anything but relaxing—at least for a while! That's often the way it is, though, when you're entering a new world. Each step of the way you will see a new side of your husband or partner developing, and you will see your children growing up right before your eyes. You will see other family members doing things that you didn't think they could—or even wanted to—do, and you will see a level of cooperation you didn't think was possible.

This new cooperation from others, however, will be different. Why? Because it will no longer be directed by you in your role as Family President. The former cooperation of other family was compliance with a command from Manager Mom. Total responsibility transfers, however, mean that the person taking over a task (child or husband) initiates and prompts the job themselves, then sequences it, monitors progress, and completes the task. You are out of the picture—and that's really different!

You will have to tolerate and encourage autonomous functioning by other people. There will be plenty of times when you'll have to bite your tongue when you see something being done "OK" but not just the way you'd like it. You'll want to criticize or correct, but—in the interest of fostering independence and motivation in others—you will remain silent. In fact, there will be times when you'll need to *praise or reinforce* that same kind of different-than-yours, only OK performance, even if it makes you squirm or even if it kills you. It's a tough but very important job. For the welfare of everyone (for the common good!), you will be working on banning parts of your old Mommy ID and creating a new Mommy ID.

Fortunately, as time goes by, there will also be moments when you'll enthusiastically applaud the changes your family is making. You'll love their newfound independence, you'll feel affection and even admiration for them, and you'll cherish the brand-new gifts you've earned through your efforts: free time and freedom from worry.

You'll cherish the brand new gifts you've earned through your efforts: free time and freedom from worry.

The Change in You

If you're going to really escape the Manager Mom Syndrome, the biggest changes of all will occur in you. You will take responsibility for yourself in a new way, just as other family members are taking responsibility for themselves in new ways. What will be required of you will be complex because it will involve changing the way you think, feel, and respond to different situations. You're going to have to be on your toes for a while, till your new way of doing things becomes more automatic (in a good way). If you recall our earlier model for human behavior, it looked like this:

A. Situation

B. Thought (appraisal of that situation)

C. Feeling or emotion (motivation)

D. Action resulting from A, B, and C

Changing your responses to different situations will require work and practice over a period of weeks and months. Here are a few examples of how your thoughts and appraisals (B), feelings and emotions (C), and good or bad behavior (D) are going to change as you move from Old Mommy ID to New Mommy ID:

Dad and Laundry: Old Mommy ID

A. Dad is carrying his laundry basket down the stairs to the washer, where he is about to do his own laundry. Two black socks drop out of the basket, and he doesn't see them.

B. Mom thinks *He can't do anything right!*

C. Mom feels resentment and frustration.

D. Mom looks irritated and says "Pick up your stuff!"

Dad and Laundry: New Mommy ID

A. Dad is carrying his laundry basket down the stairs to the washer where he is about to do his own laundry. Two black socks drop out of the basket, and he doesn't see them.

B. Mom thinks *That's really nice and it saves me time.*

C. Mom feels appreciation and affection.

D. Mom says "You're a laundry maniac!" in a friendly voice.

Shawna's Breakfast: Old Mommy ID

A. Ten-year-old Shawna is dawdling with her cereal. She should leave for school in five minutes for the ten-minute walk.

B. Mom thinks *She's goofing around again. She might be late and she'll be hungry later in the morning!*

C. Mom feels anxiety, then irritation.

D. Mom yells "Come on, honey, start eating! You have to leave in five minutes."

Shawna's Breakfast: New Mommy ID

A. Ten-year-old Shawna is dawdling with her cereal. She should leave for school in five minutes for the ten-minute walk.

B. Mom thinks *She'll eat what she wants. She can learn on her own how to do breakfast and get to school on time. She's ten. Let's see how she does. It beats me raging at her.*

C. Mom feels curiosity and anxiety reduction.

D. Mom takes another sip of coffee, then heads to the bedroom to finish dressing for work.

Jorge's Homework: Old Mommy ID

A. Twelve-year-old Jorge is playing a video game at 4:15 in the afternoon. Tomorrow is a school day. Jorge usually has homework.

B. Mom thinks *Uh-oh. What if my son doesn't remember to do his homework!? That would be terrible!*

C. Mom feels a strong burst of apprehension.

D. Mom snaps and says "Jorge, you have homework? Better get moving!"

Jorge's Homework: New Mommy ID

A. Twelve-year-old Jorge is playing a video game at 4:15 in the afternoon. Tomorrow is a school day. Jorge usually has homework.

B. Mom thinks *Jorge cares about his school work and likes his teacher. I'll keep quiet and let him handle this.*

C. Mom feels slight anxiety, but also confidence that her decision is right.

D. Mom says nothing.

Len's Scrambled Eggs: Old Mommy ID

A. Fourteen-year-old Len is making breakfast on Saturday morning for the family. He is cracking the eggs with a fork instead of breaking them on the side of the frying pan.

B. Mom thinks *Oh no. What if he gets pieces of shell in the eggs? That's not the right way to crack eggs.*

C. Mom feels anxiety and a little irritation.

D. Mom blurts out "Let me show you how to do that. You're gonna get shells in the eggs."

Len's Scrambled Eggs: New Mommy ID

A. Fourteen-year-old Len is making breakfast on Saturday morning for the family. He is cracking the eggs with a fork instead of breaking them on the side of the frying pan.

B. Mom thinks *If he gets shell in the eggs, no big deal. It's his way of doing it. Maybe it works just as good as cracking the eggs on the side of the pan. He's done it before.*

C. Mom feels anxiety followed by self-reassurance.

D. Mom says "You're getting to be a master chef! I'm hungry." She goes back to reading the paper.

As time goes by, former Manager Moms become more self-aware, and they also become more sensitive to how their automatic talking *demotivates* family members. They drop more and more of their President, Servant, and First Responder roles in different situations. And, as time goes by, kids and dads pick up more of the slack,

As time goes by, kids and dads pick up more of the slack, and they get rewarded for that change.

and they get rewarded for that change, both by appreciative mothers and also by their own appreciative selves. Their self-esteem benefits as they contribute more to the common good and operate more and more independently. Win-win-win.

The Final Two Obstacles

Former Manager Moms will tell you that the last two barriers on the road to emancipation are kind of unexpected. They are often, surprisingly, efficiency and sadness.

Efficiency—or the ferocious desire for efficiency—pops its head up frequently and also dies a slow death during an anti–Manager Mom Syndrome campaign. A charter member of the Mommy ID Ten Commandments, the President's desire to get things done now and get them done right is a goal that is very hard to shake. When Dad fumbles with the baby bottle, Riley isn't eating her breakfast, Amelia is heading down the wrong grocery aisle at 5:45 p.m., or Lucas isn't out of bed at 6:45 a.m., moms often feel (and say!): "It's just easier if I do it myself!"

It's understandably tough, especially in these days of the frantic modern family and rush, rush. What to do? Take a deep breath and review the four higher goods: personal affection, a fair distribution of labor, kids' autonomy, and—ultimately—Mom's mental health.

How does sadness fit in? I've been in the psychotherapy business for many years. When a patient or client who has been struggling with anxiety or depression or other personal problems gets better, starts feeling good, and learns how to manage their life on their own, it's a time for celebration. But it's also a time for sadness, because they don't need my services anymore and it's time to say goodbye. I've been through that transition hundreds of times. Parenting is the same. As your kids get older and more competent (with your help!), they don't need your "services" as much, and not being needed as much or in the same ways can be tough, even though you don't have to say goodbye. What to do? You focus on the competence and independence of your children, and you celebrate a job well done by both of you.

Former Manager Moms will tell you that the last two barriers on the road to emancipation are kind of unexpected. They are often, surprisingly, efficiency and sadness.

The Future

Imagine coming home from work, taking a short nap, then sitting down to look at possible vacation sites on your iPad while your daughter, Tabitha, contentedly cooks dinner for the family: sloppy joes, fresh steamed broccoli, and sliced cantaloupe. What about your Mommy ID? No problem. You got a new one a long time ago.

What are you going to do with your new free time?

Notes

1   G. R. Patterson, "Mothers: The Unacknowledged Victims," *Monographs of the Society for Research in Child Development Monograph* 45, no. 5 (1980): 1–64.

2   Arlie Hochschild, *The Second Shift: Working Families and the Revolution at Home* (New York: Penguin, 2012).

3   Gemma Hartley, *Fed Up: Emotional Labor, Women, and the Way Forward* (New York: HarperOne, 2018), 112.

4   Frank Newport and Joy Wilke, "Desire for Children Still Norm in U.S.," Gallup, September 25, 2013, https://news.gallup.com/poll/164618/desire-children-norm.aspx.

5   "Age Divorce Statistics." Date accessed July 14, 2019. http://www.divorcestatistics.org/.

6   Dorothy Tennov, *Love and Limerence: The Experience of Being in Love* (New York: Stein and Day, 1979), 41–48.

7   Jean M. Twenge, W. Keith Campbell, and Craig A. Foster, "Parenthood and Marital Satisfaction: A Meta-Analytic Review," *Journal of Marriage and Family* 65, no.3 (2003): 574–83.

8   Susan M. McHale and Ted L. Huston, "The Effect of the Transition to Parenthood on the Marriage Relationship: A Longitudinal Study," *Journal of Family Issues* 6, no. 4 (1985): 409–33.

9   Daniel Kahneman, et al., "Toward National Well-Being Accounts," *American Economic Review* 94, no. 2 (2004): 432, in Jennifer Senior, *All Joy and No Fun* (New York: Ecco, 2014), 5.

10 Matthew Killingsworth, interview by Jennifer Senior, February 6, 2013, in Jennifer Senior, *All Joy and No Fun* (New York: Ecco, 2014).

11 William Doherty, interview with Jennifer Senior, January 26, 2011, in Jennifer Senior, *All Joy and No Fun* (New York: Ecco, 2014).

12 Hochschild, *The Second Shift*, 3.

13 Alexander Szalai (ed.), *The Use of Time: Daily Activities of Urban And Suburban Populations in Twelve Countries* (The Hague: Mouton, 1972), in Hochschild, 3.

14 Joyce F. Benenson, *Warriors and Worriers: The Survival of the Sexes* (New York: Oxford University Press, 2014), 7.

15 Amy Claxton and Maureen Perry-Jenkins, "No Fun Anymore: Leisure and Marital Quality Across the Transition to Parenthood," *Journal of Marriage and Family* 70, no. 1 (2008): 28–43.

16 "American Time Use Survey—2017 Results," United States Department of Labor, Bureau of Labor Statistics, News Release, June 28, 2018, https://www.bls.gov/news.release/pdf/atus.pdf.

17 Paul R. Amato et al., *Alone Together: How Marriage in America Is Changing* (Cambridge: Harvard University Press, 2007), 170.

18 Senior, *All Joy and No Fun*, 9.

19 Viviana A. Selizer, *Pricing the Priceless Child*: *The Changing Social Value of Children* (New York: Basic Books, 1985), 14.

20 Annette Lareau, *Unequal Childhoods: Class, Race, and Family Life* (Berkeley: University of California Press, 2003), 13.

21 A. D. Coppens et al., "Children's Initiative in Family Household Work in México," *Human Development* 57, no. 2–3, (2014): 116–130.

22 Thomas W. Phelan, PhD, *1-2-3 Magic: Effective Discipline for Children 2–12, Sixth Edition* (Naperville, IL: Sourcebooks, 2016), 200–208.

23 Kerry Patterson, et al., *Crucial Conversations: Tools for Talking When the Stakes Are High* (New York: McGraw-Hill Education, 2002).

24 "American Time Use Survey—2017 Results."

25 "American Time Use Survey—2015 Results," United States Department

of Labor, Bureau of Labor Statistics, News Release, June 24, 2016, https://www.bls.gov/news.release/archives/atus_06242016.pdf.

26 Don Aslett, *Is There Life After Housework? A Revolutionary Approach to Cutting Your Cleaning Time 75%*, 2nd ed. (Avon: MA: Adams Media, 2005).

27 Russell A. Barkley, *Taking Charge of ADHD: The Complete, Authoritative Guide for Parents*, 3rd ed. (New York: Guilford Press, 2013).

Index

E

I

independence, children's. *See* children's independence

inefficiency, 187, 226

infants. *See* babies

J

judgments, worrying about, 38

K

Kickoff Phase, 101–104, 117–119

L

laundry

    American Time Use Survey, 67

    case study, 115–120

    challenging your Mommy ID, 120, 222–223

    Mom's Declaration of Independence, 160–161

Letting Go Phase, 104–108, 120

"limerence," 3

listening, sympathetic, 107–108, 138, 161

love. *See* family bonding and affection; mom-dad relationships

M

Manager Mom Syndrome, xi–xvii, 123, 156. *See also* automatic
    talking; case studies; Equal Suffering Law; Maternal Identity;
    responsibility transfers

    commandments (mindsets) of, 38–41

    concept of, xi–xiii

About the Author

PHOTO COURTESY OF
THOMAS W. PHELAN, PhD

Thomas W. Phelan is an internationally renowned expert, author, and lecturer on child discipline and attention deficit hyperactivity disorder. A registered PhD clinical psychologist, he appears frequently on radio and TV. Dr. Phelan practices and works in the western suburbs of Chicago.

If you enjoyed
THE BEST MOMS DON'T DO IT ALL

check out these other products from Thomas W. Phelan, PhD

1-2-3 Magic
Effective Discipline for Children 2–12

1-2-3 Magic DVD
Effective Discipline for Children 2–12

More 1-2-3 Magic DVD
Encouraging Good Behavior, Independence, and Self-Esteem

1-2-3 Magic Workbook
A user-friendly, illustrated companion to the *1-2-3 Magic* book that includes case studies, self-evaluation questions, and exercises

1-2-3 Magic in the Classroom
Effective Discipline for Pre-K through Grade 8

1-2-3 Magic for Teachers DVD
Effective Classroom Discipline Pre-K through Grade 8

1-2-3 Magic for Kids
Helping Your Children Understand the New Rules

1-2-3 Magic Starter Kit
Accessories to help you get started with the 1-2-3 Magic program

Tantrums! Book and DVD
Managing Meltdowns in Public and Private

1-2-3 Magic Teen
Communicate, Connect, and Guide Your Teen to Adulthood

All About ADHD
A Family Resource for Helping Your Child Succeed with ADHD

Visit www.123magic.com

1-2-3 MAGIC
IS AMERICA'S SIMPLEST PARENTING PROGRAM!

OVER 2 MILLION COPIES SOLD

MORE THAN 2 MILLION COPIES SOLD

1-2-3

MAGIC

The New **3-Step Discipline**
for Calm, Effective,
and Happy Parenting

·············· Revised 6th Edition ··············

**THOMAS W.
PHELAN, PhD**

NATIONAL PARENTING PUBLICATIONS AWARDS **GOLD WINNER**

WHAT PARENTS ARE SAYING ABOUT 1-2-3 MAGIC:

"This book changed our lives."

"The ideas in this book work! It really is like magic! I feel like I am back in charge."

"My three-year-old has become a different little girl, and she is so much happier now."